Women's Issues
in Religious Education

CONTRIBUTORS

Ruth Floyd

Joanmarie Smith

Judith M. Dorney

Regina Coll

Janet Tanaka

Ethel Johnson

Fern M. Giltner

Harriet Miller

Women's Issues In Religious Education

Edited by
FERN M. GILTNER

Religious Education Press
Birmingham, Alabama

Library of Congress Cataloging-in-Publication Data
Main entry under title:

Women's issues in religious education.

Includes bibliographies and index.
1. Christian education—Addresses, essays, lectures.
2. Feminisms—Religious aspects—Christianity—Addresses, essays, lectures. I. Giltner, Fern M. II. Floyd, Ruth.
BV1473.W65 1985   261.8'344'07   85-14272
ISBN 0-89135-051-9

Religious Education Press, Inc.
1531 Wellington Road
Birmingham, Alabama 35209
10 9 8 7 6 5 4 3 2

Religious Education Press publishes books exclusively in religious education and in areas closely related to religious education. It is committed to enhancing and professionalizing religious education through the publication of serious, significant, and scholarly works.

PUBLISHER TO THE PROFESSION

In memory of
LANA SHERIDAN MOLLOHAN
who set me free
even in an unjust society
and
dedicated to
my husband, John
and our family and friends
who want men and women to be free
and humanity to be whole
in a more just society.

Contents

Preface

Religious education has notoriously been the responsibility of women and most professional religious educators are women. These two facts themselves have become an issue.

As women religious educators have become conscious of their role and image in religion and society, they have also become conscious of the place and image of religious education in religion and society.

Women have modeled the characteristics of nurture and dependency and have been marginal in society and religion. The call to confront society in prophetic teaching has not been seen as woman's role.

However, since religious women are now choosing to become and to model independence and authenticity they are rethinking many issues. They believe that women and religious education must be seen as a central part of religion and society and that this impacts on how and what we teach.

As women are re-visioning their concept of and call to religious education, they do not clash with other prophetic visions of religious education such as liberation theology. But they are suggesting some additional changes to be integrated into the content and history, the theory and style, the objectives and methods as we all move on.

The purpose and scope of religious education is enlarged as we include all parts of life, the whole globe, all persons, all lifestyles, and all religions in our concern for change. We are strongly affirming the earth and all creation as God's handiwork. We vision harmony and healing, care and integrative sharing rather than divisions and dualities and control in our living.

Our theory and practice builds in constant change, trust, and imagination as we live and learn. We want all to be able to live fully rather than for some to be socialized to self-emptying of worth with no freedom of choice. Women think that religious education has a present opportunity to develop new models of leadership through mutual respect for the wholeness and sacredness of every human being.

Our system will be cooperative, co-creative, mutual, open-ended and giving rather than hierarchical and competitive. We vision alternative possibilities of reciprocal structures to meet the stress of today's domination over nature and persons with its ability and knowledge to destroy all life.

We believe religious education has a great future as an advocate for inclusivity and mutuality in God's good world.

I have assembled eight original articles from educators who have written on an issue of choice and importance to them in religious education. The issues chosen do not exhaust the many issues of concern to women. Neither are they prioritized as to their importance. In fact, they are not *only* women's issues but they are *indeed* women's issues and are among those being reevaluated today in religious education.

I am delighted with the compilation and the issues chosen. I am grateful for the ability, cooperation, and spirit, even sacrifice, of the contributing educators. We did not collaborate in choosing our issues and the thinking of every writer is her own.

Some of us know each other and some have never met the others. We are a diverse group of eight religious educators. We include a minister of religious education, professors of religious education, administrators of religious education, students as religious educators, teachers and directors of religious education.

We are of different religious confessions and most of us are lay professionals. In fact, only one of us is ordained as clergy. We are from different geographic areas, different backgrounds, social classes, and lifestyles. Some of us are single and some are married, one is black and the other seven are white. Our ages span at least thirty years. Presently, we live different lifestyles and commitments. We are all educated, all religious, all women, and all feminists.

We have chosen different writing styles. Some of the articles use a standard academic writing style while some are written in a more popular genre or informal style. I did not stipulate the style of writing or any particular standard. I wanted commitment, originality, and clear communication, and I believe there are a number of ways to attain those qualities.

I did ask the writers to use inclusive terms and examples. I even asked that we not be confessional so that we would intentionally include all religions in our interpretation of religious education. Yet I found that stipulation to be more difficult than I had expected since our reflection and examples, even our knowledge, are limited and come largely from our own experience and exposure.

For instance, in writing my article about structure in institutions outside the home, I chose to use as an example the setting and experience of women in theological schools. We know there are university theological schools as well as many that are not connected with universities, the so-called "freestanding" theological schools, and that some are independent. But most are affiliated with the Christian church.

In reflecting on the structure of theological schools, I am not meaning to discuss religious education but trying to establish that women have not had a part in the structuring or development of institutions in our culture.

I have chosen Ruth Floyd's article as the first chapter in hopes of building a frame of reference. Ruth presents her story of self-discovery and consciousness-raising that led her to ordained ministry and to a new depth of spirituality and authenticity. Though our stories may not parallel Ruth's, we can, like her, dive deeply into the center of our being and surface socially empowered to live our life fully in the here and now.

Joanmarie Smith has written on the ever-present inclusive language problem. Her title, "Language Again and Still," says enough in itself. She places the issue as current and persistent. The issue is how to communicate in inclusive and caring words and images so that all have equal access to receive divine insight and justice. Joanmarie's clear and persuasive logic lifts this issue to a new level.

Judith Dorney's article on the development of young women and the responsibility of religious education completely involved me. There is a reflective and dynamic quality in her writing that makes it imperative that we waste no time in answering this challenge so that not one more generation of females is culture bound nor do they see themselves as supportive persons and learn to negate their full humanity.

Regina Coll presents the issue of peacemaking as a woman's issue. Women have long been peacemakers by role and/or nature as well as in their social and religious response. Regina is particularly interested in designing an education for peace in process as well as in offering educational content in peacemaking. She explains that educators as peaceful persons teaching peaceful living and relationships is the way of peacemaking. She leads us to see that the values taught in peaceable classrooms of children or youth result in basic peace and justice education.

The two chapters by Janet Tanaka and Ethel Johnson help persons face their complicity in oppression and violence. Where our religious tradition has not made central in practice and in teaching the ministry to the poor, the oppressed, the abused and trapped, the woman who is black or of another minority group and is in double bondage, where we as religious women have accepted the "status quo," we all have repressed change and justice. Women recognize that they too have failed to be aware of racism and classism and thus have collaborated in systemic evil discrimination. We dare not distance ourselves from reality and suffering and let others bear their burdens in silence.

Ethel Johnson has written about the joys and frustrations of black women professional religious educators. She tells of their experiences in the local church as well as of religious education in the black church. Ethel shares some of her own journey with us and thereby challenges women who seek liberation to be aware that they cannot rest until all women are free and that there is healing only in solidarity with all women.

Janet Tanaka's chapter on the role of the religious educator in preventing sexual and domestic violence makes us address an issue that we have shrunk from and about which we feel especially vulnerable and powerless.

Thanks to the women's movement of the latter part of the twentieth century, violence against women has finally been brought out into the open and aired for all to see. Janet faces the problem and discusses the misinterpretations in religious tradition that condone violence and have helped in maintaining misogyny and the discrimination of women. She encourages open and frank confrontation in acknowledging and exposing domestic violence. She challenges religious educators to openly question any religious premise that is not consistent with what we believe and want to teach about a loving and just God. She accepts the family as the basic unit of society and faith and she offers helps for family education as well as bridge-building techniques for religious education. She also introduces us to a religious center for the prevention of sexual and domestic abuse.

Harriet Miller reviews and compares developmental theory and theorists. She contends that adult development as it has been created and taught and as it has created particular values has been unbalanced. She uses Carol Gilligan's research from her book, *In a Different Voice,* and agrees that past research has not included woman's development and experience; that the theories are neither applicable to women nor balanced for society as a whole. Women have surely developed, but their values are different. Their definitions of how to be strong and successful have come through affiliation and connection. As women have developed and learned in a different manner so they teach differently. Harriet's symbolization of web-making is a more satisfying and unifying view of living than the symbol of a pyramid as a view of authority. Harriet offers educational implications for her chosen view of development.

I hope these issues whet your appetite, broaden your perspective, and clear your vision to help validate women's experience and help make possible a growth and change in society.

Women are called to be prophets and to teach prophetically. They are free and grounded in abundant grace and can no longer be bound by culture but are committed to inclusivity and integration with open-ended inquiry in our ever-widening and diverse communities of faith.

I am grateful to these women who have contributed their work to this book. I am grateful to those persons who encouraged me and spurred me on. I am grateful to the friends who typed and edited and enabled the process of this compilation. Thanks to Barbara, Reggie, Vicky, Margo, and Sue for helping and affirming me.

I am appreciative of the patience of my husband and family and friends as I have worked on the project and have not been my relational self.

I have worked through some frustrations and anger in this effort and pray for the freer world for men and women.

FERN M. GILTNER

Chapter 1

Telling My Story*

RUTH FLOYD

I was born because of a magic stone. There were probably other factors that were significant in my birth, but the magic stone is symbolic of what my birth says to the rest of my life. My parents had married in the late 1920s, and as the first child in the family, if I had been born in the early years of their marriage, my life and my theology would have been different. Instead, for ten years there were no children. The magic stone was purchased in Canada when my parents visited the birthplace of the world-famous Dionne quintuplets. The stone was a symbol of fertility, and I was born the following year.

Instead of experiencing my parents' anguish at losing their home and jobs during the depression, I was born into a period of hope and recovery. In the first five years of my life I gained a sister and brother and our happy family moved into the house that would be "home" until the death of my parents many years later. This solid, comfortable beginning was the foundation for a life that continued to expect everything to be OK even in the face of threats to that stability. I was too young to experience the war, and

*Based on the book *Diving Deep and Surfacing*, by Carol P. Christ

my father was too old to have to participate in it. Of course we experienced air raid drills and gas and food rationing, but these are more likely memories from the history books than from personal experience. My life focused around my family and neighborhood friends. My photo album records new Easter outfits, the new sled at Christmas, and days at the park or the beach. And in my eighth year there is a picture of the neighborhood children, bicycles, tricycles, and wagons decorated for a parade. I suspect we were celebrating the end of World War II. I also suspect that this was the first piece of "war news" that was directly shared with the children in our family.

It was a time to celebrate and my mother loved celebrations. I have no doubt that it was her suggestion, her crepe paper, and her American flag which inspired the children's parade. Just as it would be my suggestion, crepe paper, etc., that would result in Fourth of July parades for my children. In discussing Doris Lessing's *The Four-Gated City,* Carol P. Christ suggests that exploring the relation between mother and daughter "forces a woman to plumb the deepest levels of her experience."[1] There were many times in my life when I would not have been able to identify a relationship between my mother and myself. It has only been since my mother's death in 1977 that I have begun to identify who I am and in that process realize how much of my mother is in me. My mother was not a talker and neither was I. There are no memories of long talks through which we could discover each other. It was not until the last year of my mother's life that she told me the story of the magic Canadian stone.

Instead, our relationship was one of experience. My whole childhood revolved around family activities, or at most, the "family type" activities of scouts and Sunday School. We did things together. The importance of this is only beginning to dawn on me. There were no speeches in our house about how wrong war was. At the same time war was ravaging the world, I was learning how right love was through my own personal experience. Instead of hearing about how little we had due to shortages during the war, we celebrated what we did have. A day at the park or the beach was worth walking to the store all week in order to have the gas for the family outing. Adrienne Rich suggests that women have always "worked with what is at hand, delicately separating that which is salvageable in order to create something needed, something beautiful."[2] This is more than a description of remaking old clothes or using up leftovers in the refrigerator. My mother was an expert at taking the whole of our life and "delicately separating that which is salvageable in order to create something needed, something beautiful." Margaret Atwood's *Surfacing* describes the spiritual quest of a woman and her need to identify the gifts of the power that have been transmitted from her parents to her. I am not sure I want to differentiate between gifts and power, and yet the words do take on different meanings. From my mother comes the creative, the beautiful, the optimistic.

From my father comes the power. A strong, silent, handsome man, my father was naive in his trust of others. And that naivete was never lost. He trusted and believed in people, and those around him never considered betraying that trust. At a time when a look at the whole world could make anyone a cynic, my father looked at those around him and believed. And he loved. It has taken a very long time for me to realize how much both parents loved. It was hard to "see" the love. After marrying into and then divorcing out of the demonstrative-type family, I could finally begin to see how much more love it takes to allow each person in a family to be themselves, to discover their own

potential, to be free to make mistakes, fall away, come back
. . . and always be loved.

Sometimes it is almost impossible to comprehend how a
female growing up in such a "typical" family (which may be
more atypical than I ever realized) during the forties and
fifties could come to feel such freedom and lack of oppression. But that solid rock foundation of trust and love allowed my brother and sister and me to go off in many
directions, sometimes moving thousands of miles away
without experiencing any stifling sense of loss. We are not
what others would term a close family and yet maybe we
are bonded by the love and freedom that was our parent's
gift to us.

I do not know what my parents believed about God. At
least from the time we were school age we attended church
regularly. My father was superintendent of the Sunday
School and my mother taught Sunday School for more
years than I can remember. But if I learned anything
about God or Jesus it is either long forgotten or so deeply
ingrained that I cannot identify it. I was growing up in
Detroit, and the Methodist church I attended was in the
kind of building pictured on New England postcards: a
white church with a steeple, a sanctuary on the main floor
and a basement for Sunday School, pot-lucks, bazaars, and
children's parties. The church may have been built out in
the country, but when we attended it was surrounded by
homes on a typical city block. If I can stereotype, I suspect
that the church was a combination of small-town roots and
big-city environment. What I learned in that church did
not come out of the curriculum or the preaching. When I
was eight years old I posed for a picture with my Sunday
School class. There are people in that class that I still have
ties with. I learned stability. My parents gave fully of their
time and talents and as I was growing up I too began to

take responsibility for "my" church. I learned stewardship. I found joy and happiness in the fellowship at church and I asked my friends to join me there. I learned evangelism. Only one house separated my best friend and me. She was Catholic. We never went to school together. But I went to the Catholic Youth Organization and she went to the Methodist Youth Fellowship. I sat in the back of her church while she went to confession on Saturday morning. I helped gather flowers for the small altar she had in her bedroom. We huddled together in a corner of her porch, playing very quietly for the three hours of Good Friday afternoon. I learned ecumenism. I found encouragement and acceptance at my church. I learned about love. I doubt very much that Paul Tillich's language about the "ground of being" was used in that church. But my grounding is certainly in that church and in my family. Carol Christ says at the end of *Diving Deep and Surfacing* that when we recognize the grounding of our lives "in the ground of being, women's spiritual quest gives women the strength to create alternatives to personal relationships and social institutions where women's value is not recognized."[3] Somehow, by some quirk of fate, act of God, or coincidence, I believe I was fortunate to grow up in an environment that grounded my life "in the powers of being that often leads to newfound self-awareness and self-confidence."[4]

Before this begins to sound like the story of Mary Poppins or some other perfect and unreal story, several points need to be made. Most of the story I have told so far can only be told within thirty to forty years of hindsight. I did not know I was getting such a strong grounding. I thought I was quiet, insecure, not very pretty, a follower, and sometimes unloved. I do not believe I was fully tuned in to my family and the people around me. The shock of being usurped of my place as the center of my family after only fifteen months and then (in my mind) losing even more when my brother was born when I had just turned five years old, probably caused me to shut down some feelings at the same time I developed some independence. With two younger children in the family, I took on the responsibility of looking out for myself. The reality of the situation is probably somewhere between this independence and the sense of total security I had in my family.

Another thing is just because a person is firmly grounded and there is the possibility for self-awareness and self-confidence, it does not automatically happen. As a young woman, I was also a product of my time. My parents were very intelligent people, but I don't believe my father finished high school, and graduation from high school was the end of my mother's formal education. Yet it was assumed the three children would go college. It was also assumed that my sister and I could choose between becoming a nurse or a teacher. Even though an aptitude test showed me high in mechanical ability (another gift from my father), there was no other option open to me. Since I did not do too well at the sight of blood, I went to college to be a teacher. Drawing on Kate Chopin's book, *Awakening*, Carol Christ quotes Chopin as describing Edna's spiritual quest in "a series of steps, small at first, that move her far beyond the conventional woman's life she had known."[5] I began my series of steps. While still living at home, I enrolled at the local university to learn how to be a teacher. I taught Sunday School and did some individual tutoring as part of some kind of freshman student teaching experience. Not much of a step and yet a start. For the first time I had friends from other parts of the city. Before that my friends had all come from my neighborhood or my church. My school friends were also my church friends.

And then I took a real step. Actually somebody pushed

me. Scholarships were not available for average students like myself and so I needed to work. I was lucky enough to get a job at the university that would adjust to my school schedule. I was trained on a small switchboard and became a receptionist for a new department at the school. That was not the step. I was pushed when a member of the faculty needed someone to operate a piece of equipment in this new department and no one was available but the receptionist. So one afternoon in 1955 I was trained and that evening I was operating a television camera. Educational television was being born in Detroit and I was in on its birth. New worlds open up new opportunities. We were not concerned with whether jobs were available for women in commercial television. At the university both men's and women's creativity were allowed to expand. There were no rules, no unions, no "this is the way it has always been done," and, incidentally, hardly any audience.

That was the end of my education courses. I began taking every media class I could. I was a good camera "man" (this was in the fifties) and I was even better on the audio-board, coordinating microphones, turntables, and tape decks (maybe that high-school aptitude test was not so far off). Where were the men who could be threatened by the women entering this field? They were not at Wayne State University. Faculty encouraged us, including visiting faculty from local commercial television stations. We were not male and female students—we were all in this new experience together. No oppression, only opportunity for creativity—thank you fate/God/coincidence.

But then the real world: In my second year at the university I fell in love with a fellow student, we were married at school midyear and I was six months pregnant by the end of the school year. My husband got the jobs in television, I took care of the baby . . . and fifteen months later another baby. I was diving deep. The Korean War had come and gone while I lived the carefree life of a teenager in the fifties. The Vietnam War went on and on while I was sinking lower and lower into self-negation and self-hatred. On the outside I was a good mother, I was creative, a good homemaker and wife. On the inside I cried, I felt lost, unloved. I cooked, I sewed, I gave the best parties, I did Cub Scouts, Brownies, etc., yet something was missing. I did not realize this at the time, so I felt very guilty for being so unhappy (I wonder what my mother's life was really like?). I tried going back to school but my husband's schedule changed and I had to drop out because he would not be available to babysit and the car would not be available. More tears, a few hesitant attempts at taking a step on my own, but always diving deeper. When I realized how much I was sinking while on the surface I appeared to be floating, I wonder how many women around me were drowning while making all kinds of waves.

Darkness and light ebb and flow in waves over seventeen years of marriage. That "nothingness . . . a vague sense of anxiety"[6] is there but cannot be identified. Memories of this time are of myself out working, associating, relating to people in a real world or of myself existing at home in an unreal world. "A certain light was beginning to dawn dimly. . . the light which, showing the way, forbids it."[7] I could not face it. Carol Christ says, "the 'dark night' is a metaphor for the sense of emptiness felt by those who have broken their ties with conventional sources of value but have not yet discovered their grounding in new sources."[8] She says the "experience of nothingness is liberating" but it is only liberating as "women reject conventional solutions and question the meaning of their lives, thus opening themselves to the revelation of deeper sources of power and value."[9] I was not yet ready to reject the conventional solutions.

And at the same time I was experiencing the nothingness of the marriage relationship. I was also beginning to realize myself as a creative, constructive person. I had begun to do youth work at my church and for the first time felt strongly about the value in what I was doing. No amount of conflict with my husband could convince me that what I was doing at the church every Sunday morning and evening was wrong. I can identify closely with Edna's "first direct challenge to the tacit premise of their marriage—his authority."[10] What was simply a continuing expression of power by the man became a monumental step into the light when the woman defies that authority. Edna "was beginning to realize her position in the universe as a human being, and to recognize her relations as an individual to the world within her and about her."[11] So was I.

I have two mental pictures of myself during this time. One is of a creative, energized person, coordinating a youth program involving fifty or sixty youth and adults. The other picture is of a tired, bored, aching person curled up under a blanket, sitting all alone in a cocoon and thinking—and waiting. One picture would not survive without the other. The energized person in the church created the frightened person at home as the contrast between being and nonbeing was shown to be so great. The frightened person at home would have crawled further into her cocoon if it had not been for the challenge of the people at church. I was still trying the conventional solutions. I pretended like everything was OK. I kept busy. I signed up for a Yoga class. And finally I approached a counselor.

Again, thank fate/God/coincidence. When my marriage ended I was surrounded by a very supportive church community. I was working with a pastoral counselor. And I had developed a pattern of exercise and meditation that modified the anger and anxiety to a manageable level. The five or six months after my husband moved out are in some ways a blank period in my life. But at least twice a week during that time I met with the counselor and told my story. "In sharing experiences and stories, women learn to value themselves, to recognize stagnant and destructive patterns in their lives, to name their strengths, and to begin to take responsibility for their lives." Christ quotes Ntozake Shange's play, *for colored girls who have considered suicide/when the rainbow is enuf,* as Shange envisions black women "born again on the far side of nothingness." Like the black women Shange portrayed, I was being "born again on the far side of nothingness."[12]

That period of my life is like a many-petaled flower blossoming on slow-motion film. Slowly, I was moving "through self-negation and self-hatred to new affirmations of selfhood, power, and responsibility."[13] Like the woman in *Martha Quest,* even though I suffered from not having an image of self, I had a capacity within myself that enabled me to survive the experience of nothingness.[14] That capacity came from the roots of my growing and was nurtured by the community of my church and my family.

How did I get from the tightly closed bud to a fully open blossom ready to face whatever the world had to offer? I wish I knew. When I see someone diving deep, I wish I could invoke the magic formula that would bring instant awareness and growth. Of course that is impossible. What I can do is share my story. There have been many times when a word or two of my story has opened up another woman's quest. "When one woman puts her experience into words, another woman who has kept silent, afraid of what others will think, can find validation."[15] I cannot say to a hurting person, "God loves you, you don't need to hurt." I can tell that person how I have come to love myself enough to survive that hurt. And I can love that person. That is how I learned about God's love. Nobody told me, or at least I never heard the words. But people showed me; they loved me while I hurt.

So much learning and growth went on at that time that it is hard to sort out and identify. And many years later I find it amazing that there is still so much to learn. One of the first things I was able to do was to affirm my self as a person. To love myself. This was a fairly easy step because there had nearly always been parts of my life that did this. Deep within me was my strength, and when I was able to recognize the power my husband had exerted causing me to bury my self I was able to allow that strength to surface again. "A decision to put her relation to her self ahead of her relation to a man is not easy for a woman who has been brought up on the myth of love, a female salvation myth. But it is a decision women must make (at least symbolically) if they are to pursue the interior journey."[16]

In "Trying to Talk with a Man," Adrienne Rich writes "of nothingness in a relationship with a man." And even though I was experiencing that nothingness, I was also being affirmed in my "somethingness" by others. This enabled me to face the possibility of being alone. Like in Rich's poem, I began to realize that "the feared state of being a woman without a man might be easier than the frustration of living with one whose life runs on a different course from her own."[17]

No one wants to be alone or lonely. My life revolved around people, but my life had also become anchored in my home and my husband. When the anchor was pulled up I had no idea where I might drift. I had never looked at my life apart from my family. It was not until four years after I became single that I actually had to face living alone. In those four years I began to have confidence in myself as an individual, not as my husband's wife or my children's mother. As I completed my undergraduate degree I learned about myself through career planning exercises, assertiveness training, and practicing counseling skills. I remember one counseling class session where we listed ten things that were important to us, and then we were asked to rate them in degree of importance. Then we looked at what would be left of ourselves as each of these things was removed. I discovered that even if I lost my house, my job, and my children—even if I lost virtually everything around me—I still felt I would exist. There was something within me that could not be taken away. Carol Christ says that "if a woman has experienced the grounding of her quest in powers of being that are larger than her own personal will, this knowledge can support her when her own personal determination falters."[18] I could not name the powers of being within myself and yet larger than myself, but I could name many of the things that were not powerful.

I had spent a great deal of my life, as the song says, "looking for love in all the wrong places." Searching to have my selfhood confirmed by the love of others. On good days now I can be like the woman alone that Rich writes about: "the woman who has chosen, not solitude, but the possibility of solitude, in choosing to be who she is—a woman no longer desperate for the love of others because she loves herself."[19] Because there is still so far to go, I still look for love and approval from others. But like the women in Shange's choreopoem, I will not be likely again to deny the pain of my relationships. I may or may not be able to find that one person to love me, but I "can at least refuse to be a victim, and this is an important step."[20] Because I love myself now "I chose to love this time for once/with all my intelligence." In Rich's poem "Splittings," "to love with intelligence is contrasted with loving out of infantile need, and it affirms both lover and beloved as separate adult persons."[21]

Carol Christ writes of woman's quest as moving from nothingness to awakening. In "awakening" women move "from conventional notions of the meaning of life to a more direct experience of the "really real" or ground of being, from ordinary to extraordinary consciousness, from bondage to freedom."[22] It is in this awakening that women refuse to be a victim, resolve to love intelligently, learn to trust the "capacity to grow and learn from any situation."[23] As in *Martha Quest,* "it does not matter where she goes or what she does as long as she maintains contact with that core of herself, which is the location of her capacity for insight."[24]

It seems almost impossible to describe this awakening experience without the sense of power, or empowerment, that it implies. When a woman discovers her own sense of self-identity, an identity that has not been dictated by men and the culture created by men, this is a gaining of power—"the power that comes from being oneself and expressing one's perception of the world."[25] When that power is recognized as within the self, and also as larger than self, Carol Christ names them " 'great powers'—the self's sense that it is related to something larger."[26] In *Mr. God This is Anna,* Anna discovers God "in my middle," and in *for colored girls who have considered suicide/when the rainbow is enuf,* the woman in red cries, "i found god in myself/ & i loved her/i loved her fiercely."[27] There is a power that wells up from within when a woman can recognize God within herself. This "finding God in herself is an acknowledgment of her self's grounding in larger powers."[28]

What is it that makes a God that is a "ground of being" so much more attuned to women than the heavenly Father above? Aside from the obvious problems with a patriarchal God, there is the solidness, the firmness of the ground and women's long ties with nature, agriculture, and creation. "Grounding expresses the notion that the self is not only oriented to great powers, but it is also supported by them just as the ground provides a place on which to stand."[29] Recently, in meditating on a series of slides and photographs I found myself closely relating to pictures of trees and paths through the woods. While other people would be climbing the mountains, I would be searching out the sunny spot on the ground beside a lake. As I looked again at my photograph album the pictures I have kept of myself are those taken outdoors and even sitting or lying on the ground. There is something that draws me to the firmness of the ground and the strength of a "ground of being."

The woman's quest which may move from nothingness to awakening then might possibly inspire mystical insight. And again woman's ties with nature are often sources of mystical experiences. Carol Christ believes that women may be more apt to come to a mystical experience out of their nothingness. "Women never have what male mystics must strive to give up. Mystic insight may therefore be easier for women to achieve than men."[30] Not only do women have less to lose, they are certainly open to the possibility of an experience that "shatters an old self." But women need to be affirmed in the possibilities of mystical experiences.

Women are observers. They know how people relate by observing. They may sense something is wrong. Doris Lessing calls Martha "a watcher," which "allows her to step back, to assess."[31] She talks about how "a person can know something and yet not know it in a meaningful way."[32] It is possible to have a transcendent experience and because the only thing surrounding that experience is a sense of nothingness, the transcendence is forgotten. "Not remembering transcendent experiences is a common human problem, but it is intensified for women who have no stories, models, or guides to remind them of what they knew."[33]

How true this is. My story could not become a story without the stories that have come before me. One of the memories I have of my elementary school is of the days we went to the school library. I would automatically head for the table near the "biography" shelf. I think I may have read nearly every one of those stories of people. I have graduated beyond the elementary versions of Davy Crockett and Helen Keller's life stories, but I have never stopped wanting to hear people's stories. Like Martha in *Martha's Quest,* I "use books to verify. . . insights, to confirm something I know or half know."[34] But how few of those stories were really women's stories. How can I relate to the life of Queen Victoria or Jenny Churchill? And yet I think even these stories have been important in my growth as a woman, because of that gift from my mother of "delicately separating that which is salvageable in order to create something needed, something beautiful."[35] Even in the stories of great and famous women I would grasp the truths that I knew and yet did not quite know in a meaningful way.

But where are the stories of women's mystical experiences? They are not on the elementary biography book shelves. And they are not readily available in the popular literature. When mystical experiences are part of the story they are likely to be associated with witches or goddesses. I think of Erica Jong's novel, *Fanny.* Although this is the story of an eighteenth-century woman, her experiences with a coven of witches and Goddess worship were my first insight into the stories that Carol Ochs and Elaine Pagels present in historical context. *The Mists of Avalon* is an interesting novel that explores the struggle between mysticism and early Christianity. In the story of *Sally Hemings*, Thomas Jefferson's slave and companion, she had mystical experiences which are explained only because she is a black woman slave. The fact that she was educated in France and the United States by Jefferson is not related to her mysticism.

Until I read Carol Christ's four characteristics of mysticism, I never would have believed I had had such experiences. But again, when someone tells her story, my story can be told. Following a night of diving deepest, my vision of the next day is brighter than any sunshine I can remember. In the middle of the night I had challenged my husband to either come home immediately or never come home again. I spent the rest of the night crying hysterically. He did not come home. The next day we had had a counseling appointment. I went alone. When I told my counselor how I had become so angry that I had screamed and yelled and thrown something across the room, he congratulated me! I had shown real anger for the first time. I was still concerned for my husband, and I asked a friend to find out if he was all right. While I waited to hear news of my husband, I cleaned house for the first time in weeks. I opened drapes and windows and let light in to my cocoon after a long, dark winter. When my friend came to the house and told me that my husband was OK but he would not be coming home, I was given a hug, told that I was loved, and then I was left standing alone in my kitchen. My memory of that moment is bathed in sunlight and fresh air. I had lived through the nothingness, had faced the dark night of my soul and there was now a fleeting "sense of illumination, revelation, or awakening." I did not identify these feelings at the time, but that moment is in my memory now, clearly with the sensation of "being grasped or held by a superior power."[36] Like Kate Chopin's *Awakening*, I felt as if I "had been trying to make out clear shapes in a dark room and suddenly the lights were turned on."[37] I always thought that was a strange way to experience the moment when I realized seventeen years of marriage were over. Now, I believe I can understand the movement from nothingness to awakening that was marked by this mystical experience.

"While mystical experiences in nature frequently provide women with a sense of authentic selfhood, many also have mystical experiences in society or community."[38] Although the memory of my experience is one of sunlight and fresh air, the role that my counselor and my friend played in that day are an indication of the importance of community for me. One reason I never thought of myself as a mystic is that I had pictures of hibernating in a cave in the wilderness in order for solitude to bring mysticism.

Woman's spiritual awakening needs the social support of a community. Women need to recognize and name their powers. Together they can learn "to value everything about being a woman." "The new celebration of women's bodies, powers, solitude, and connection with each other is the beginning of the end of centuries-old patterns of self-hatred and self-negation."[39] Women's spiritual freedom is not complete until that can be translated into new possibilities in her life and relationships with others.

My own spiritual quest allowed me to be open to the new awareness that would come my way. I can see now that the spiritual quest can only go so far before it must become a social quest: "a struggle to gain respect, equality, and freedom in society—in work, in politics, and in relationships with women, men and children."[40] In this way "women's spiritual quest provides new visions of individual and shared power than can inspire a transformation of culture and society."[41]

This is my story—it goes on—and hopefully grows ever closer to the true ground of my being—which I call God.

NOTES

1. Carol P. Christ, *Diving Deep and Surfacing* (Boston: Beacon Press, 1980), p. 63.
2. Ibid., p. 78.
3. Ibid., p. 131.
4. Ibid., p. 21.
5. Ibid., p. 31.
6. Ibid., p. 29.
7. Ibid., p. 29.
8. Ibid., p. 14.
9. Ibid., p. 13.
10. Ibid., p. 32.
11. Ibid., p. 29.
12. Ibid., p. 98.
13. Ibid., p. 19.
14. Ibid., p. 56.
15. Ibid., p. 23.
16. Ibid., p. 64.
17. Ibid., p. 77.
18. Ibid., p. 11.
19. Ibid., pp. 85-86.
20. Ibid., p. 113.
21. Ibid., p. 90.
22. Ibid., p. 18.
23. Ibid., p. 69.
24. Ibid., p. 69.
25. Ibid., p. xic.
26. Ibid., p. 10.
27. Ibid., p. 117
28. Ibid.
29. Ibid., p. 10.
30. Ibid., p. 18.
31. Ibid., p. 56.
32. Ibid.
33. Ibid.
34. Ibid., p. 71.
35. Ibid., p. 78.
36. Ibid., p. 20.
37. Ibid., p. 18.
38. Ibid., p. 38.
39. Ibid., p. 24.
40. Ibid., p. 8.
41. Ibid., p. 131.

Chapter 2

Language Again and Still

JOANMARIE SMITH

Introduction

Our notion of the divine is fundamental to any religious
education. For millennia that notion has been pervasively
male regardless of the religion. Although most people recognize that God is not *really* male, the very use of the term
"God" betrays that realization. God is defined as a male
deity. To demonstrate to students the idolatrous hold on
their psyche of this maleness, I ask them to replace the
word "God" in their prayers and references with "Goddess" for just thirty days. They invariably find it a difficult
to impossible task.

I do not mean to replace the male idolatry with a female
idolatry. But as a tree that is unhealthily bent too far in one
direction has to be bent for a while in the extremely opposite direction before it can assume its proper heavenward
stance, so, I believe, we must go to similar extremes in
order to authentically experience what the mystics have
always told us: The deity is "not this, not this, not this . . ."

The identification of maleness with the deity is not only
a religious issue however; it is also a political issue. Where
God is male, male is God. It is no coincidence that the

27

millennia in which we have worshiped a male-like deity is also the millennia in which we have worshiped males as specifically godlike. This system has been called patriarchy. More recently it has been called sexist. It has had the effect of women being considered, and worse of considering themselves, less worthy, less human, and ungodlike.

One can attempt to correct this situation in one of two ways: from above, that is, to try to demasculinize our image of the divine[1] or from below, that is, to try to root out the sexism in society. In this article I take the second approach.

Attention!

The expression, "First, you have to get their attention," has universal application in any educational situation. But it seems to be especially necessary when dealing with the topic of sexism. Most people are aware of the issue and have formed an opinion and a position. Unfortunately, more often than not the opinion and the position are that the problem is no longer an issue, or if it is, it is a trivial one. I suggest to educators therefore, that they come at the problem from another route rather than attack it head-on. I suggest that they use consciousness-raising experiences. In order to gather your own data you might consider a dry run before working with larger groups.

Try these exercises with your family, the persons with whom you work, or those to whom you minister—preferably *not* in a situation where they suspect that you are trying to educate them to feminism.

1. Ask the boys and girls in your circle what they would like to be when they grow up. Then ask them what they would like to be if they were the opposite sex.

2. Ask young women would they mind taking the name of their husbands when they marry. Ask young men would they flip a coin (or use some similar method) to determine whose name both husband and wife would use after marriage.

3. Use three different groups. Ask the first group to list the qualities of a mature person. Ask the second to list the qualities of a mature man, and the third to list the qualities of a mature woman.

If your findings correspond with mine you will discover more often than not:

1. That when girls are asked what they would want to do if they were boys, they elevate the conventional prestige of their choice. So, for example, if as a girl they wanted to be nurses, as boys they might want to become doctors. Boys, on the other hand, often seem to find it almost impossible to think of themselves as girls and many answer simply, "Nothing."

2. Some young women would not mind using their husband's name. Some would even prefer it or demand it. But it is the rare, rare young man who can contemplate even the *risk* of giving up his surname for the rest of his life. It is good to do this exercise in mixed company because it demonstrates to the females in the group how crucial at least half the world's population thinks one's name is to one's identity.

3. There will be a greater correspondence between the lists of mature persons and mature men than between mature persons and mature women.

Why? Why are the inequities of a patriarchal culture still being internalized by our young people? Feminists have argued for the last twenty years that our sexist language has contributed to, if not constituted, the situation.[2] Yet, concentrated efforts to "clean up" our language have apparently not been sufficiently profound or extensive. There is still and again a need to address the issue of sexist language.

As recently as last quarter I received a term paper from a seminary student with these lead paragraphs:

> In the writing of this paper I have found it necessary to use a personal pronoun to refer to the term "student." I have chosen to use the masculine pronoun to serve this function. Let it be understood that this pronoun is used in its generic sense; it refers equally to both male and female. I have chosen this route over the alternative of using the compound pronoun "he/she" because I find this alternative to be grossly unesthetic.
>
> If you observe any sexual inequality in the content of this paper because of the use of the masculine pronoun, then you are in error due to the above statement.

How could an intelligent, sensitive, mainline churchman still harbor such sentiments? All the major denominations have begun to revamp the language in their worship and their educational texts, haven't they? What is the problem?

The problem, as I see it, is that in many instances the change to inclusive language reflects a *concession*, not a conviction. People get tired and bored and impatient with concessions. Meanwhile the tired and bored and impatient conceders fuel their dis-ease by reading the exclusive, sexist language in such socializing instruments and arbiters of literary taste as *The New York Times, Time, Newsweek* and by watching and/or listening to major television and radio networks. Someone has said that it takes almost five years for convinced feminists to flush the sexism from their language. It is imperative, therefore, that we work to *convince* the *conceders* of the necessity for inclusive language. This article will outline the strategy of such an effort.

I will lay out theory and data to convince the conceders. Perhaps if enough persons in the influential field of religious education can stimulate conviction among those they influence, such a hue and cry will be raised that we will eliminate sexist language forever, contribute to the permanent elimination of sexism, and restore the deity to women.

Forests and Falling Trees

Almost everyone remembers the question from Philosophy 101: "Does the tree falling in the forest make a noise if there are no ears to hear it?" Remarkably few persons, however, remember the answer, "No."

Introductory philosophy students fight that one. They sense, correctly I think, that their notion of the hard objectivity of reality is threatened in that answer. The most compelling evidence I offer to demonstrate the validity of the "No" is the transistor. I whip out a transistor radio and run through the AM and FM bands on it. Were these conversations and this music in the room before I turned on the radio? Of course, but it was the instrument of the radio that made them accessible to us. I remind them that there are all kinds of television programs dancing around outside their heads too. If we had the proper instrument, we could make them visibly present to us. In other words, a sensation requires both a stimulus and a sensor. The falling tree is certainly a stimulus, but if there are no sensors, or receivers, or, in this case, ears, there is no sound. A sensation without a stimulus is an hallucination. A sensation without a sensor is like a square circle; one can talk about it, but it cannot exist.

The next thesis is more immediately relevant to the issue of language. Raw sensations do not exist either. That is, what we call a sensation is always "cooked" by interpretation. An uninterpreted sensation is not experienced. The term "experience" describes our interaction with reality. There are also two required ingredients to experience: sensation and interpretation. Another way of putting it: We cannot say what we *see;* we can only say what we *think.* For example, what do you see below?

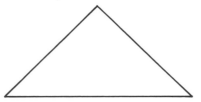

If you answer, "A triangle," I remind you that triangle is a very sophisticated mathematical concept. You cannot possibly *see* a triangle. Nor can you *see* lines and angles. And while "black and white" or "ink on a page" is not so sophisticated as the mathematical terms, they are still concepts, ideas. You cannot say what you see apart from these concepts because you *cannot see* apart from these ideas. If you do not have the concept you do not see it. But language is the form with which we conceptualize.

Persons whose sight is restored after being born blind report that they do not see *things* but only a blur of color. They have to be taught or socialized into connecting the colors they see with the ideas and definitions they have learned.

Alan Watts says that reality is like a great mishmash over which we throw a netting that marks off reality into manageable pieces.[3] It is like the netting of longitudinal and latitudinal lines we throw over our planet so that we know where we are at any point and can share that information with others. Blind persons know all about the netting, but they have not seen it fitted over the reality of color. The netting *and* the color, or sound, or touch, or taste, or smell constitute our experience of reality.

Definitions, Meanings, and Images

We define reality. We put the endings *(finis)* or boundaries, or netting on reality. We agree on the elements of a definition so that if I say "chair" you know that I am talking about a piece of furniture on which one person can sit.

Meaning, however, is not at all the same as definition. The meaning of something is the difference it makes. So, for example, the definition of electricity is a charge of energy. But the meaning of electricity is that we can watch the Olympic Games while they are taking place no matter where they are. We can eat meat that we purchased a year ago. We can read books all through the night and we can be cool in the summer and warm in the winter. All the differences that electricity makes possible constitute the meaning of electricity.

Images are something else again. Images are the energy of language. They are the fuel of meanings. Images are usually reflected in the connotations of language—the feeling that certain words give us. Images usually account for the differences (the meanings) words or expressions have in our society.

Peter Berger says that reality is maintained by conversation.[4] The image I get is of a volleyball game. In conversation we keep aloft the definitions and meanings that structure a society. We maintain a society by using the same words in the same way. When someone lets the ball drop or refuses for one reason or another to use a word or recognize a meaning that has been kept afloat in conversation, a crisis of some kind is introduced into the tissues of society.

When Rosa Parks refused to agree to the *meaning* of Negro, that is, one who rides in the back of the bus, a restructuring of society began that is still not completed, unfortunately. Similarly, with the word *black*. I taught in an all-black school in the 1950s when the term *black* was still an epithet. Then that community turned the word inside out. They said in effect, "We are not going to use that word anymore in a pejorative way in which it has been used in the conversation of this society. We are going to let that ball drop. From now on, black is beautiful." And they pulled it off, although we are still stripping the old meanings from our conversation as in black humor when it means "sick humor" or blacklisted and blackballed.

The definitions of "Negro" and "black" were neutral enough, but the meanings and images were another story. If we want to see where women are in society we need only look at the terms that define them and then think of the meanings these terms have and the images they convey. It is especially revealing to examine some parallel terms applied to men and women. In almost every case, the male term really is neutral or even favorable, but the female equivalent has some unseemly connotations.

An unmarried man in our society is a bachelor; an unmarried woman is a spinster or an old maid. The female equivalent of master is mistress, and Burke's Peerage tells us that the equivalent of "sir" is "madam."

To be called a wizard is quite complimentary, but to be called a witch is another story. For a girl to be called a tomboy is not so bad, but for a boy to be called a sissy can be devastating. The female equivalent of "Chip off the Old Block" has only negative suggestions; it is "Mama's Boy."

Until recently there was no female equivalent of "mister" which designates a man in his own right. The analogous terms were "Miss" and "Mrs." They were not and are not equivalent to mister, however, because they did not refer to the person but to her relationship, or lack of one, to a man. Undoubtedly one can think of other examples. I cite these because the case I want to make is that if our society is structured by meanings, by the difference something makes, then women in society have been and still are to a great extent not quite human.

We have been told and are still being told by some that "men" is generic, that its definition includes both male and female human persons. This smacks of ideology which is defined sociologically as a rationale proposed by those in power which enables them to retain power. Alma Graham states the problem clearly by putting it in more abstract terms.

> If you have a group half of whose members are A's and half of whose members are B's, and if you call the group C, then A's and B's may be equal members of group C. But if you call the group A, there is no way that B's can be equal to A's within it. The A's will always be the rule and the B's will always be the exception—the subgroup, the subspecies, the outsiders.[5]

Men = Human

"Men" is not generic on a bathroom door. If it ever was generic, it has not been so in the history of our nation. The use of "men" and "mankind" in the United States has had the effect of socializing us to males as the norm of the *really* human.

The opening words of our sacred document, "The Declaration of Independence," offers irrefutable evidence: "We hold these truths to be self-evident, that all men are created equal, that they are endowed by their Creator with certain unalienable rights, that among these are Life, Liberty, and the pursuit of Happiness."

Not even all men were referred to. Black men were not, nor were uneducated men with no property. We subsequently computed that black men were exactly two-fifths less than white men, but for all practical purposes, women did not exist.

A hundred years later little had changed. So ingrained was the image that Men = Human that even when inclusive language was used, it made no difference. The Fourteenth Amendment ratified in 1868 reads in part:

> All persons born or naturalized in the United States and subject to the jurisdiction thereof are citizens of the United States and state wherein they reside. No state shall abridge the privileges or immunities of citizens of the United States.

One would think that everyone could now vote? Certainly in federal elections everyone could vote if "men" is generic. They could not, of course.

Because black men were still unable to vote in many of the Southern states another amendment was introduced and ratified within two years. The Fifteenth Amendment was worded quite simply:

> The right of citizens to vote shall not be denied or abridged by the United States, or by any state on account of race, color, or previous condition of servitude.

How much more specific did one have to be to guarantee the vote for women? Very. It took another half-century before women were permitted to vote in every state of the union.

Some women in 1870 tried to act as if "citizen" included them, as if it meant that they too were entitled to vote in the 1872 presidential election. In one instance, Susan B. Anthony actually persuaded registrars in Rochester, New York, to accept her vote. She was quickly indicted because she "knowingly, wrongfully and unlawfully voted for a representative to the Congress of the United States."[6]

There were a number of irregularities at her trial. She was not permitted to testify, the jury enlisted for the trial was not permitted to judge the issue, and she was fined for speaking at her sentencing. The jury of her peers was, of course, garnered from the voting roles and therefore all were males.

A similar case made it to the Supreme Court in 1874. A unanimous decision was handed down in *Minor* vs. *Happersett* which explained to Virginia Minor that Mr. Happersett of St. Louis, who had refused to register her, had acted correctly. The opinion held that Mrs. Minor was a citizen of course, but so were children, the insane, and criminals, and the states were obviously within their rights withholding suffrage from them! Ergo . . .[7]

How much better is the situation today? Would-be law students who sought scholarship funds offered to aid and assist worthy and ambitious young men to acquire a legal education were told that they did not qualify because they were not men. At about the same time the charter of a local Kiwanis Club was revoked. The members had interpreted the term "men" in the bylaws of the organization as generic and had therefore invited women into their membership. But "men" was not generic for the leadership of the Kiwanis Club. What power we give to anyone whom we allow to include us in or out!

If there is any doubt that the attempt to use "men" as generic has had the effect of establishing males as the norm of what it means to be human, think of the use of feminine endings. How does a statuette compare to a statue? Most of our agent words are neuter: leader, doctor, teacher, professor. The suffixes "er" and "or" mean simply, "one who." To put other endings, so-called feminine endings, on so many of these agent words such as actress, or aviatrix, or poetess, reinforces the image of male as the standard. Where these endings have not been used we see that "male as norm" still subtly informs our consciousness. So, for example, we speak of doctors and women doctors, or journalists and women journalists.

If, by changing our words, we can change reality, that seems to be a cheap price to pay for justice. But perhaps it is just the apparent ease with which it can be done that makes so many people disregard or trivialize the suggested change. Or perhaps there is some intuition that the change is not so cheap or easy.

No change is easy—and those changes which disrupt the unconscious structuring of our lives as language does seem especially threatening. I have noticed that even when seats are not assigned in a church or classroom, people almost invariably and repeatedly sit in the same general area. As an exercise in changing perspective, I sometimes ask students to switch from that general area. They do—and they get the point, but they wish I had simply described the exercise, and they continue in their new places with some dis-ease.

If changing one's habitual physical position for so brief a time as a class period has this admittedly slight but palpably disturbing effect, what is the cost of requiring a change of the habitual linguistic structure of a psyche?

Every revolution which attempted to change radically the existing reality has used language to implement and sustain that revolution. John Adams presided for days over congressional deliberations about how the new president should be addressed. To get the impact of what was involved, compare the expression "Mr. President" with the honorifics of address used for those titles we retained from our European background: Your Excellency (Governor), Your Honor (Mayor and Judge). The French revolutionaries tried to equalize the population by calling everyone "citizen" as have the Soviets with their use of "comrade." In the Civil Rights Movement of the sixties the blacks *named themselves* in an effort finally to be seen by a culture that had kept them invisible despite constitutional amendments that made them citizens and gave them the right to vote.

This is what feminists want: to have names. They do not want their identity subsumed under the so-called generic "men" and "he." They do not want simply to be seen solely in terms of their relationship or nonrelationship to a man. They want simply to *be*.

This is a religious issue because when anyone is treated as less than human it is a religious issue. Elohim created one species, Ad-ham, which comes in two basic models (Gen. 1:27), but in numberless shapes, colors, and sizes.[8] When this truth is realized (made real) and incorporated (embodied) in our culture the pervasive male imagery will begin to collapse. The recognition that *both* female and male image the deity may dawn universally. Then, not only will women be seen, but they will see in themselves the image of the divine so long withheld from them. Then they may have experiences similar to that of the poet Ntozake Shange.[9]

i found god in myself
& i loved her / i loved her fiercely

NOTES

1. This approach is used in Joanmarie Smith, "Hen, Homemaker and Goddess," *PACE* (December, 1983).
2. Casey Miller and Kate Swift have done the most definitive work in this area. See their *Words and Women* (Garden City, New York: Doubleday, 1976) and *The Handbook of Nonsexist Writing* (New York: Lippencott and Crowell, 1980).
3. Alan Watts, *The Book on the Taboo Against Knowing Who You Are* (New York: Vintage Books, 1972), p. 52.

4. Peter Berger, *The Sacred Canopy* (Garden City, N.Y.: Doubleday, 1967).
5. Alma Graham, Letter to the Editor, *The Columbia Forum* (Fall, 1974).
6. Eleanor Flexnor, *Century of Struggle* (Cambridge, Mass.: Harvard University Press, 1959), pp. 169-171.
7. *Minor* vs. *Happersett*, 21 Wall (U.S.), 162 (1875).
8. See Phyllis Tribble, *God and the Rhetoric of Sexuality* (Philadelphia: Fortress Press, 1978) for a thorough exposition of Gen. 1:27.
9. Ntozake Shange, *for colored girls who have considered suicide / when the rainbow is enuf* (New York: Macmillan, 1975).

Chapter 3

Religious Education and the Development of Young Women

JUDITH A. DORNEY

"If women are to be made restless and questing . . . they must be made so through education."

—Margaret Mead

In 1969, Dr. Florence Howe wrote an essay in which she asked the question, "Why do we educate women?"[1] In 1981, Jean Marie Hiesberger in her essay, "The Ultimate Religious Education Challenge," asked "how one raised a child religiously."[2] Today, I would echo and restate the questions of both women, for as a religious educator I believe we must address ourselves specifically to the issue of the religious education of young women.

I do not think we can assume that this question has been sufficiently dealt with in either the history of educational thought or in the field of religious education. As Jane Roland Martin discovered when she began to reflect on Rousseau's treatment of the education of Emile and Sophie:

The sad truth is that historians of educational thought have ignored not only Rousseau's sex bias, but the whole topic of

41

the education of women. They have neglected Sophie because they have implicitly defined their subject matter as the education of male human beings, rather than the education of all human beings.[3]

Until recently we find this same inattentiveness to women in work done on moral development. In her work with young people and with women facing a decision about abortion, Carol Gilligan heard women defining the issues and their approaches to them differently than the boys and men who had historically been used as the subjects of such research. Her findings that a woman's voice is not better or worse but different is an event whose shock waves are just beginning to be felt. One very important recognition in her work is that what has always been assumed to be the norm, i.e., white, male experience, is not.

At this point the question of why we educate women might be better asked: What do women learn and how does this affect their lives? I would suggest that the language, the texts, the models presented, the teacher's own attitudes, and the kind of interaction that takes place with students are among the things that influence what young women learn. Because this language, these texts, and the models presented frequently have assumed that white male experience is the norm, girls and young women learn that their voices and experiences are not important. Thus their schooling contributes to their diminished sense of self-esteem.

When we raise these questions with regard to religious education the concerns are enlarged. Cognizant of the fact that most of the theology which is taught has been developed solely by men of Western culture, we realize that once again the "norm" as well as notions of goodness, justice, God, sexuality, etc., have been determined and promoted by and for a very small segment of the world's population. Valerie Saiving critiques these theologians' definition of love as

> completely self-giving, taking no thought for its own interests but seeking only the good of the other. . . . Love makes no value judgments concerning the other's worth; it demands neither merit in the other nor recompense for itself but gives itself freely, fully, and without calculation. Love is unconditional forgiveness.[4]

One of the problems of this interpretation is pointed out by James Nelson:

> Christian teaching too often has had enormous difficulty distinguishing between creative self-love and selfishness. Too frequently they have been equated without the realization that egotism and selfishness arise from inadequate self-acceptance rather than too much of it. As a result the familiar polemic against selfishness can undermine, unwittingly, that self-acceptance which is integral to genuine faith and outgoing love. Women in particular have suffered, socialized into derivative identities and nurtured in the supposed virtue of giving without receiving. The all too frequent result is the tendency to cling to self-negation as if too much affirmation and success would depress them. This is one of the tragedies of sexist dualism.[5]

Consequently, "both as woman and as a Christian she regards it as natural to defer to others, to serve, to think of herself last, to cut larger pieces of pie for her husband and sons. It is so ingrained a behavior that is seems to be part of her nature."[6]

Clearly multiple problems arise for women because of the content of such messages. Three problems which affect women in a particular way are poverty, domestic violence, and a stunted spiritual development. In commenting briefly on each the relationship between how women live and what they learn about themselves should become clearer.

Girls and young women are far too often schooled toward dependency. As they learn that their ideas and experience are not as important as men's, as their own self-image is weakened, they learn to attach themselves to those who are perceived to be more capable and valuable. In so doing they often surrender much of the responsibility for their lives to these men. Such a pattern is disastrous. But as already indicated, women cannot be held solely responsible for these choices. They are most often acting on what they have learned about themselves. Although "we educate women as if there will always be someone around to take care of them,"[7] we are not preparing them for the reality of their lives. "Nine out of ten girls presently in high school will work (outside the home) during their lives. If they marry, they will work an average of 25 years, if they do not, they will work an average of 45 years."[8] Since we do not educate women to develop the skills they will need to support themselves or their families, and since much of the work done by women is not valued, monetarily at least, the result is that women and their children are the poorest of the poor.

This unhappy fact is supported by a study of the U.S. National Advisory Council for Economic Opportunities published in 1980. It predicts that by the year 2000, 100 percent of America's poor will be women and their children unless social policy is changed. It further states that of the over 12 million full-time workers who are eligible for public assistance, 67 percent are women and that in 1981 the poverty rate for female householders was more than three times that of male householders and five times that for husband-wife families.[9]

Domestic violence is a serious crime in which women and children are again most often the victims. There are a variety of reasons why domestic violence occurs, but in the

particular case of wife abuse the victim frequently offers
two reasons why she was willing or compelled to remain in
the violent situation. One reason is that the woman somehow felt that she deserved the beatings, the other is no
economic alternative. It is appropriate to mention however,
that for many women their religious upbringing has contributed to an unwillingness to leave the situation of abuse.
Religion has promoted the

> value that the family must be preserved at all costs. "Till death
> do us part" has sometimes meant death to women. A Christian
> counselor of battered women believes that the Christian image
> of the suffering servant—suffering for others—had adversely
> affected wives who find themselves in a situation of being beat-
> en by their husbands. Again and again women report that they
> have gone to their clergymen for help in such situations only to
> be told to "offer it up" or "try to forgive him." The emphasis is
> on saving the marriage rather than protecting the life and limb
> of the woman being abused.[10]

When we educate women toward dependence their
spiritual development is also inhibited. Again, contributing
to this problem are traditional religious ideas on who the
good woman is. Of course underlying this notion are the
patriarchal perceptions of goodness and woman. But if we
recognize that Christian spiritual development should be
understood in light of total human development

> the problematic nature of women's spiritual development be-
> gins to be recognized. Because women are often thought to be
> naturally self-effacing and dedicated, the deeply problematic
> effects of the way women are conditioned to their behavior are
> overlooked. Recent studies show that women's behavior that is
> praised as virtuous (i.e., loving) and mature (i.e., other direct-
> ed) is actually often behavior symptomatic of severe immatur-
> ity. . . . Women are led to believe they are virtuous when
> actually they have not taken the necessary possession of their

lives to have an authentic "self" to give in self-donating love. They are often praised as holy when they are still spiritually dwarfed.[11]

Such grevious offenses against women must be addressed. When we become aware that at least a portion of these problems results from what women learn about themselves and themselves in relation to men, we must ask, not whether religious education must address these concerns, but how. Religious education must, among other things, be education for justice and as such must help people to "emerge from their silence, find their voice and become fully conscious subjects, capable of trying to change the conditions in which they live."[12]

It is appropriate to wonder how religious education might do this. The remainder of this essay is devoted to just such an exploration. My comments will be most appropriate to a high-school religious education curriculum. However, I believe they can be adapted to a variety of situations. My initial remarks will be general in terms of resources and particular topics. Following this, three units have been developed which deal with Images of God, Images of Woman, Images of Society/World. These units as described are most usable with a class of young women but can be and have been used in a coeducational setting with slight revision.

Resources

One general resource I recommend for all high-school religious educators is the book *Faith and Sexism,* by Marianne Sawicki. She touches on many of the topics that religious educators deal with and makes suggestions as to how one might teach them in a nonsexist way. The topics include: God, sacraments, grace, sin, morality, saints, church, Jesus, creation, Holy Spirit, death.

In church history and scripture courses there needs to be a recovery of the voice and experience of women. The work of and the roles played by women in this history must be presented to students. To continue to neglect or ignore women's voices in this history is to contribute to the silencing of women today. This is no small task for the religious educator who often must search for these women her/himself. However, I cannot overestimate the importance of introducing young women to their foremothers. Women begin to view themselves and other women differently as a result of learning about the significant women of their faith history. Two helpful resources in this area are: *Foremothers*, by Janice Nunnally-Cox, which identifies and informs about the women of Israel, the women of Jesus' time, and the women of the early church; and *Women of Spirit*, edited by Rosemary Radford Ruether and Eleanor McLaughlin, which begins with the women of the early Christian communities and brings us into the present experience of women in the Jewish and Christian traditions. *In Memory of Her*, by Elizabeth Schüssler Fiorenza, is an excellent resource for the teacher. Here she offers a feminist reconstruction of early Christian theology and history. It is a powerful example of the kind of uncovering of women's voice and experience which must continue to take place. These women cannot be presented as an aside to what was "really" happening but must be presented seriously as people who contributed to the shape of the church. Furthermore, where the contributions of women have been lost to us, examination must be made as to why and be looked at in light of the culture of the time so that students can gain an understanding of how the structures and attitudes of a society can promote or impede certain movement.

Many courses in a religious education curriculum deal with the topic of love. This is certainly a challenge for any teacher to deal with, but I believe it quite necessary to offer a variety of ways for describing love. Often the words of 1 Corinthians are used as the model of love, "Love is patient and kind; love is not jealous or boastful; it is not arrogant or rude. . . . Love bears all things, believes all things, hopes all things, endures all things" (1 Cor. 13:4-7). This is certainly *a* valid definition of love. It is *a* model but one that would be better presented alongside other thoughts on love. For example, Beverly Harrison writes about the place of anger in the work of love. She says,

> Anger is not the opposite of love. It is better understood as a feeling-signal that *all is not well* in our relation to other persons or groups or to the world around us. Anger is *a mode of connectedness* to others and it is always *a vivid form of caring.* . . . Anger directly expressed is a mode of taking the other seriously, of caring.[13]

Of course one must examine how to caringly express anger, but how important this idea could be for the adolescent whose love for her parents is often fraught with anger. This insight can also be very meaningful for those relationships in which one senses something is wrong but does not want to upset or disturb anyone involved. The connection of service and love is important, but it should be clear that the "service of Christ is a calling to be instruments of God's help, not a calling to be subservient . . . service that perpetuates dependency is not service at all."[14] Love must be examined then by teacher and students in the context of different relationships with serious effort to discern what a life lived in true love of self, others, and the world means and how anger might be a catalyst for growth in relationships.

Courses that deal with personal morality focus some attention on sin. Here too there is a need to look at what/ whose definition is being used and what/whose experience is being reflected. Valerie Saiving enlightens the issue by pointing to the fact that the "identification of sin with pride, will to power, exploitation, self-assertiveness, and the treatment of others as objects rather than persons"[15] is a definition coming out of male experience. She suggests that the temptations of women are more likely to be

> triviality, distractibility and diffuseness, lack of an organizing center or focus; dependence on others for one's own self-definition; tolerance at the expense of standards of excellence; inability to respect the boundaries of privacy; sentimentality, gossipy sociability and mistrust of reason—in short, under-development or negation of the self.[16]

Letty Russell voices the idea that submission is sin, for in submission "women refuse to accept their full created status as partners with men in the work of God's mission in the world."[17] The work of Carol Gilligan can also serve as an important reminder to us that the male idea/ideal can no longer be considered normative for everyone. Our concepts and teaching of sin and grace must begin to reflect this. Sexism as sin must also be uncovered. This tremendous challenge is posed by Daniel Maguire who argues that

> sexism is the elementary human sin. If the essential human molecule is dyadic male/female, the perversion of one part of the dyad perverts the other. And to distort femininity and masculinity, the constitutive ingredients of humanity, is to distort humanity itself; nothing will be spared the fallout from so radical a corruption. Here is original sin.[18]

The power of this notion is evident and can also have impact on our teaching of sexuality and what it means to be female and male in the image of God.

Two resources I recommend as companions to looking at sexuality and woman's experience are *Seasons of Woman*, edited by Penelope Washbourne, and *Daughters in High*

School, edited by Frieda Singer. *Seasons of Woman* presents a multicultural patchwork of songs, poems, prose, and pictures reflecting woman's physical/emotional/spiritual development. *Daughters in High School* is an anthology of work by high-school women dealing with such areas as roles, relationships, and questioning. Both can also be valuable in exploring women's spirituality.

Having offered these general recommendations I shall turn to the task of presenting the three units referred to above. Each unit can be presented in a variety of courses; however, as I begin each description I shall comment on where each has been used.

Images of God

This unit can easily be presented in a course on faith or prayer. The lessons examine who God is and how our relationship with that God affects our lives. This really is a crucial unit as our image(s) of God do influence how we see ourselves, others, and our world as well as how we act toward ourselves, others, and our world.

Although we recognize that our images of God are inadequate or limited, we also recognize that our religious tradition has given us some very dominant images of God. The images that have been handed down to us are primarily male and/or hierarchal images.

Aware that people need "appropriable images" of God, Maria Harris suggests that the task for a religious educator is to ask, "Why these images? On what grounds have we incorporated them? Shall they remain central? Who will benefit and who will lose if such critical examinations occur? Will anyone benefit? Will anyone lose?"[19] Such questions are of particular importance to young women as one of the results of being presented with a God who is always other than herself is that it requires a greater leap of the imagination to find God within herself. "It actually can alienate a woman from her own experience when she presumes the 'Holy' is not at all like herself."[20]

To begin the students are asked to write a description or draw a picture of their God and when finished these descriptions are to be shared with the class. Attention should be drawn to the characteristics of God which are described. Following the sharing of descriptions there should be a discussion of such questions as: Were there any dominant or prevailing images of God? If so, why did these images dominate/prevail? Why did each describe God as she did? Where did these images come from? What was left out of their descriptions? Why? Do any of the descriptions surprise them? If so, which ones and why? If not, why not?

The next activity is to image God as an animal. This lesson is also primarily discussion as an examination takes place of "what kind of animal would God be?" Close attention must again be paid to the qualities of the chosen animals for that will tell more clearly how the students see God. Also, students should be encouraged to look for any connection between the animal they chose and their original description of God. They should then be asked how they relate to a God who has these qualities. Is that descriptive of the way they presently relate to God? Why/why not? If not, why do they think they chose that animal?

An exploration of several different scriptural images of God follows the animal imaging. The students are instructed to locate these scripture passages and determine what God is being compared to:

Luke 15:11-32	Forgiving father
Isaiah 66:9	Woman giving birth
Isaiah 66:13	Mother comforting son
Isaiah 28:26	Teacher

1 John 1:5	Light
1 John 4:8, 16	Love
Psalms 22:9-11	Midwife
Psalms 36:7	Bird

After clarifying problematic passages there is discussion of their reactions to these images: Are they familiar with any of them? If so, which ones and why? If not, why not? Do they think they are good/appropriate images of God? Why/why not? What can each image tell us about God? Which is their favorite? Why?

Next on the agenda is an examination of some historical and contemporary images of God. These are distributed to the students on a worksheet and they are asked to describe how God is like each one of these images. They include God as: "Dwelling, spouse, food, friend, head, sister, brother,"[21] "mother and father,"[22] "ray of darkness, sea pacific,"[23] "incomprehensible desert, essential light,"[24] "a great ear at the heart of the universe hearing human beings into speech—to new creation,"[25] "the inner spirit, the inner voice, the human compulsion when deeply distressed to seek healing . . . within ourselves."[26] After discussing how God is like these images, the students are reminded that these are images of God presented in our religious tradition and as images they can tell us something about God. However, we must be careful not to identify the image as God or we shall be limiting God.

It is now appropriate to look at how the students can image God. An "Analogy Worksheet"[27] is distributed which asks each student to create her own image of God and list the ways that God is like that analogy. This is helpful as it gets the students to imagine God for themselves, and it reminds them that these are, after all, just images. Also they are participating in the tradition by doing what the Scripture writers and others have done. After having the students do two analogies each, each member of the class shares one. This can be reminiscent of a litany as each one reads a different analogy.

The following activity is based on a short story by Alice Walker.[28] An explanation is given to the students about how frequently people are able to find or see God within themselves. For example, during the years of slavery in this country many of the slaves found God healing them from within when they were at their lowest points. The class is then assigned reading about some of the women who had such experiences (i.e., Harriet Tubman, Sojourner Truth). The reading is followed by a written reflection on their lives as if they were those women. They are then asked to write a description of the God they found within. Certain of these would be shared with the class. One value of this kind of exercise is that it can help students begin to see that God is within them as well as within others who are different from them. At this point it is important to look with the students at what this tells us about God, ourselves, and each other.

A similar objective may be served by using poetry or music which describes a discovery of God (life, healing, the Holy) within one's self. If the students have ever had such an experience they are asked to write about it and how it made them feel. Again, what does it say to them about God? About themselves? If students have never had such an experience, they are asked to write an explanation of why they think that is so. Also, is there anything that the class or church can do to promote such an experience and sense of God within? This written work is shared only with the student's permission.

The closing lesson consists of the students working in groups to make a collage of God.[29] The collages should include images we have explored as a class as well as any others they may want to add. Comparison is made with the first description of God they had to write and conclusions are drawn by the class as to what they have learned of God, themselves, and others as well as what this means for relationship with God, self, and other.

Images of Woman

This unit can be offered in a vartiety of courses, i.e., personal morality/social justice or relationships. The purpose is to spend some time reflecting critically with the students on who defines them, how they are defined, what the implications of these definitions are on woman's self-image and lifestyle, and what they think of this. Advertising, music, and poetry are the primary resources.

The first task is to ask the students to be attentive to advertising which appears on television, in magazines, on billboards, etc. Students should record what advertising they see/hear and what the image of woman is that is presented in each. This assignment could last from a few days to a week. Of course the longer amount of time they have for observation the more thorough will be the findings. Students should also be encouraged to bring in ads they see for the class to analyze. Their observations of the images found should be discussed as well as inquiry into how they felt about them. Such questions can be included in the discussion: Did they feel they were accurate representations of women? How many women do they know like that? If they are not all accurate, whose ideas were they? What attitudes about women were conveyed in this message? What was the purpose of projecting that particular image? Who would benefit from this image and who would suffer? How?

Following this discussion of the images of women in advertising is an exploration of images of women in music and poetry. Two of the songs mentioned here have been popular with young people within the last year. However, other songs more current and popular may be substituted.

"She Must Be Somebody's Baby"[30] has been recorded by Jackson Brown. After listening to the words together students are asked to consider their reactions to the song: What does it mean to be somebody's baby? Is it desirable to be somebody's baby? Why/why not? Is this imagery used for men? Does it mean or imply the same thing? What is the woman's relationship to the man like in the song? What does this suggest for her relationships with other women?

The second song, "The Girl Is Mine,"[31] is recorded by Michael Jackson and Paul McCartney. In this recording the two men argue/discuss who "owns" the girl. Questions which can be explored here are: Is it important to be somebody's girl? Why/why not? Do they see it as desirable that the two men argue over this girl? Toward the end of the song the two men simply exchange statements such as: "The girl is mine." "No, she's mine." "No, she's mine." "The girl is mine." What imagery does that suggest to the student? (The record cover inside the album illustrates this with the woman being pulled by each man from either side.) What role does the "girl" have in determining who she will be with? Each man says that the "girl" has told him he is the only one for her. What does this say about her truthfulness?

In contrast to these two songs, Holly Near has recorded a song in which she confesses to a friend that it's more important that they stay friends rather than fight over a man. "It's More Important To Me"[32] can follow "The Girl Is Mine" and the different values presented in each brought out.

In using women's poetry to contrast with the music, Alice Walker's poem, "Be Nobody's Darling," is appropriate. Some of the same questions can be examined in terms of the image of woman being presented. In one of her television interviews Alice Walker prefaced her reading of this poem by saying that she was addressing young women:

> Be nobody's darling;
> Be an outcast.
> Take the contradictions
> Of your life
> And wrap around
> You like a shawl,
> To parry stones
> To keep you warm.[33]

How do these words compare with those of Jackson Brown, Michael Jackson, Paul McCartney, and Holly Near? What is she asking women to do? Do the students think women want this? Why/why not? Do they want to do this? If a woman was "nobody's darling" would she be an outcast? If so, why do they think that is the case?

Hadewijch, a thirteenth-century woman, belonged to an independent community of women, the Beguines. Her poem, "To Live Out What I Am," offers another voice for examination.

> My distress is great and unknown to men
> They are cruel to me, for they wish to dissuade me
> From all the forces of Love urge me to.
> They do not understand it, and I cannot explain it to them.
> I must live out what I am;
> What Love counsels my spirit
> In this is my being; for this I will do my best
> . . . What use is it for me to force my nature?
> For my nature shall always remain
> What it is and conquer what belongs to it
> However men may narrow its path.[34]

How does this poem compare with Alice Walker's and with the three recordings? What do the students see Hadewijch to be saying and how might she say that today? What might she be trying to live out and how did men narrow the path for women in that time? Does this happen today? If they do not see this happening today, why not? (Recalling the advertising may help to stimulate discussion on this.)

The final poem to be used here is "Meditation on Luke I," by Dorothee Sölle, in which she interprets the Magnificat for today. The students are first encouraged to look at the Mary who is presented here. What are some of the characteristics of the woman who said these words and what does that suggest to them about the kind of woman Mary of Nazareth might have been? Where would she fit into the music and poetry just looked at? How might each of the artists examined respond to this poem? What would women be like in this new situation? How might relationships between women and men be different? Do they see this as a possibility for themselves? Why/why not? What would have to change in the world for this new way of being to be brought about? How might such changes begin? Do they see signs of such change? It is important to point out here that this is a reflection on Scripture and that in the Lucan Magnificat Mary is proclaiming what God wants. The students are asked to consider why God might want such a change for women and ultimately for the world.

Finally the students are asked to reflect on themselves and their relationship to each of the images presented in advertising, music, and poetry. Which do they think they are most like? Why? Are they happy there? Why/why not? If not, where would they like to be? What are the advantages and disadvantages of each situation? Which women do they take more seriously? Why? Returning to Sölle's poem to close this unit the students are asked, How can we help each other to reach "the land of freedom" where "the empty faces of women will be filled with life" and "we will become human beings long awaited by the generations sacrificed before us?"[35]

Images of Society/World

This unit seems most appropriate to a course dealing with social justice or one which examines systemic/social sin. A specific introduction to the unit is not essential as the purpose becomes clear in its unfolding. In fact the unit can be used as a way to help the students clarify their vision of how society/world should be in light of their religious tradition. It can also lead into an explanation of why the world may not be as it should be.

The unit begins with an exercise from *Education for Justice: A Participant Workbook*.[36] The exercise is "spaceship survival." Briefly, the task is that the earth is going to be destroyed and the spaceship you are in may make ten landings to rescue ten people. The students are given the following instructions to help them decide who to save.

> Section A lists 22 nationalities and Section B lists 20 professions. Choose a nationality and write it in front of the person you want to spare, e.g., Filipino worker. You may use the same nationality as often as you wish, but you must choose ten different people according to their professions.[37]

The earth is going to be destroyed so the students must understand that their ten choices would be the sole survivors and bearers of the world as they would like to see it.

Once the students have made their choices they should be examined in terms of why they chose, in what combinations, and why. Some time should be given to looking at why they chose those they did. Did they choose from knowledge or ignorance? This discussion leads into the part of the unit that needs more time, that is, who was not chosen and why. Were these choices of who to exclude made out of knowledge or ignorance? What kind of world were they trying to preserve? Would their choices preserve it in that way? What are their assumptions about those not chosen?

In looking at who were chosen and who were left out the students are asked to reflect on what experiences in their lives led them to make the choices they did. They are asked to look at their own experience of being in the world as a student, a citizen, a church member, a family member, a media watcher, etc. Whose experience is seen as authoritative? Whose experience determines how decisions will be made? Even as texts and resources? What do those texts and resources include and exclude?

The students are then asked to make a list of the "silenced"—those whose voices are not regularly heard, those whose experience is not drawn upon. Invariably the list includes children, women, old people, poor people, women and men of color, people who are part of the world outside of the United States and Western Europe, disabled people, etc. Exploration is made into why these silences exist. *Silences,* by Tillie Olsen, is one of the resources used here. Her work parallels the idea just expressed that certain people have been silenced in terms of the work of creation. It is a valuable book, and within it are many whose voices have been heard but who mourn for those voices which have been lost to us:

> What has humanity not lost by suppression and subjection? We have a Shakespeare; but what of the possible Shakespeares we might have had who passed their lives from youth upward brewing current wine and making pastries for fat country squires to eat, with no glimpse of the freedoms of life and

action . . . stifled out without one line written, simply because, being of the weaker sex, life gave no room for action and grasp on life?[38]

I have no patience with the dreadful idea that whatever you have in you has to come out, that you can't suppress true talent. People can be destroyed; they can be bent, distorted and completely crippled. . . . In spite of all the poetry, all the philosophy to the contrary, we are not really masters of our fate. We don't really direct our lives unaided and unobstructed. Our being is subject to all the chances of life.[39]

Here it is appropriate to ask the students what Tillie Olsen asks herself and her readers. "What's wrong in the world then, that it doesn't ask—and make it possible—for people to raise and contribute the best that is in them?"[40] What are the structures, situations, that prevent this from happening? While exploring such questions, however, it is necessary to look at what the "silenced" have been doing (while being "silent").

Women understand—only women altogether—what a dreary will-o'the-wisp is this old, common, I had almost said common-place, experience, "when the fall sewing is done, when the baby can walk, when house cleaning is over, when the company has gone" . . . then I will write the poem, or learn the language, or study the great charity, or master the symphony; then I will act, dare, dream, become.[41]

This is my social life . . . I run around the city and stand in line. . . . I stand in line for medicine, for food, for glasses, for the cards to get pills; I stand in line to see people who never see who I am; at the hotels, sometimes I even have to stand in line to go to the john. . . . These agencies they have to make it as hard for you to get help as they can, so only really strong people like me can survive. All the rest die standing in line.[42]

(After three hours of standing in line for food stamps, Letty found she didn't qualify because she didn't have cooking facilities in her room.)

These two women suggest what the silenced have been doing while others are deciding policy, writing texts, and defining morality. Raising questions about the silences should make it possible to begin to uncover the reasons for the silences and these should be examined in light of the kind of vision offered in our religious tradition. "When things are put right, humanity and all the creatures of the earth will be in harmony."[43] Students and teacher must consider what must be done for things to be put right and for this harmony of life to be brought about.

In identifying and locating the "silenced," a search must be made for ways of acting both individually and corporately so that these voices can be heard. One very immediate suggestion that is made for the young women in the class is that they take themselves seriously and become more responsible for themselves. This means "refusing to let others do your thinking, talking, and naming for you; it means learning to respect and use your own brains and instincts, hence grappling with hard work."[44] It means refusing to be silenced!

Final Suggestion

My final suggestion for the teacher is that we must be willing to critique ourselves. These attitudes we have learned through time and institutions die hard. We must look not only at the material we deal with but also at the people and the structures of the educational institution itself. What attitudes do we have toward our women students, and, if we teach men, what is our attitude toward the men? How do we relate/react to the wo/men we teach? Do we give more credence to the ideas of either group? How do they relate with each other in the classroom? Do the men dominate socially, verbally, actively? Adrienne Rich advises the teacher to:

Look at a classroom. Look at the many kinds of women's faces, postures, expressions. Listen to the women's voices. Listen to the silences, the unasked questions, the blanks. Listen to the small soft voices, often courageously trying to speak up, voices of women taught early that tones of confidence, challenge, anger, or assertiveness are strident and unfeminine. . . . Look at the faces of the silent, and of those who speak. Listen for a woman groping for language in which to express what is in her mind, sensing that the terms of academic discourse are not her language.[45]

Whose experience do we draw upon when teaching? Who writes the texts? Do we make an effort to present as many voices as we can when presenting our material? Are we as demanding of our women students as we are of our men students? Do we somehow entertain the idea that the women do not have to be as successful and disciplined because their future really depends on another anyway? Are we a part of school activity which presents different messages to women and men? Are young men asked to set up chairs, empty garbage, carry text books from room to room, while the young women are asked to deliver the mail, dust the bookshelves, help decorate the room? As teachers even our classroom management carries messages to the students. I believe this self-examination as teacher is no simple undertaking. It is constant and in my experience a long-term endeavor. I am still discovering how subtle these experiences of discrimination between men and women students can be. It requires vigilance for the teacher who wishes to overcome the learned assumptions of our culture.

In closing I must simply assert that this issue is so serious and so basic that it challenges religious education at its roots. To paraphrase the words of Mary Kay Thompson Tetreault, "The process of including women's voices and experiences in our teaching does not simply mean adding materials to traditional religious education materials. It means rethinking how much of how religious education is done."[46] As religious educators we must make the commitment to join hands, heads, and hearts in our efforts to uncover the explicit and implicit sexism in our curricula and carve out new ways of doing religious education which will nurture young women and young men toward wholeness.

NOTES

1. Florence Howe, "The Education of Women," in *And Jill Came Tumbling Down,* ed. Judith Stacey et al. (New York: Dell, 1984), p. 74.
2. Jean Marie Hiesberger, "The Ultimate Religious Education Challenge," *Religious Education* 76, No. 4 (July-August, 1981), p. 355.
3. Jane Roland Martin, "Sophie and Emile: A Case Study of Sex Bias in the History of Educational Thought," *Harvard Educational Review* 51, No. 3 (August, 1981), p. 371.
4. Valerie Saiving, "The Human Situation: A Feminine View," *Womanspirit Rising,* ed. Carol Christ and Judith Plaskow (New York: Harper & Row, 1979), p. 26.
5. James Nelson, *Embodiment* (Minneapolis: Augsburg, 1978), p. 65.
6. Mary Bader Papa, *Christian Feminism* (Chicago: Fides/Claretian, 1981), p. 59.
7. Rita Bornstein, "The Education of Women: Protection or Liberation?" *Educational Leadership* 36, No. 5 (February, 1979), p. 334.
8. Ibid.
9. Jill Craing, "US Women: Hardship or Hope," *Network* 11, No. 4 (July-August, 1983), p. 12.
10. Papa, *Christian Feminism,* p. 95-96.
11. Joann Wolski Conn, "Women's Spirituality: Restriction and Reconstruction," *Cross Currents* (Fall, 1980), pp. 293-95.
12. Brian Wren, *Education for Justice* (New York: Orbis Books, 1982), p. 7.
13. Beverly W. Harrison, "The Power of Anger in the Work of Love," *Union Seminary Quarterly Review* XXXVI (Supplementary 1981), pp. 49-50.
14. Letty Russell, *Human Liberation in a Feminist Perspective* (Philadelphia: Westminster Press, 1974), p. 30.
15. Saiving, "The Human Situation: A Feminine View," p. 35.
16. Ibid., p. 37.

17. Russell, *Human Liberation in a Feminist Perspective*, p. 144.
18. Daniel Maguire, "The Feminization of God and Ethics," *Christianity and Crisis* (March 15, 1982), p. 59.
19. Maria Harris, "Prayer and Vision: Part 1: The Imaginal Vision," *PACE* 10 (1979), p. 5.
20. Conn, "Women's Spirituality: Restriction and Reconstruction," p. 297.
21. John Chrysostom's images of God cited by Eleanor McLaughlin in "Christ My Mother: Feminine Naming and Metaphor in Medieval Spirituality," *St. Luke's Journal of Theology* XVIII, No. 4 (September 1975), p. 232.
22. Juliana of Norwich, *Revelations of Divine Love* (New York: Doubleday, 1977), p. 187.
23. Catherine of Siena's images of God cited by Kathleen R. Fischer in *The Inner Rainbow* (New York: Paulist Press, 1983), p. 117.
24. Images of God attributed to the German Mystics, *The Inner Rainbow*, p. 117.
25. Nelle Morton, quoted by Susan Griffin in *Rape: The Power of Consciousness* (New York: Harper & Row, 1979), p. 42.
26. Alice Walker, "A Letter of the Times," *Ms.* (October, 1981), p. 63.
27. Katheryn Piccard, "Analogy Worksheet," 1979.
28. Walker, "A Letter of the Times," p. 63-64.
29. Linda Clark, Marian Ronan, Eleanor Walker, *Image-Breaking; Image-Building* (New York: Pilgrim House, 1981), p. 20.
30. Jackson Brown, Danny Kortchmar, "Somebody's Baby," Electra/Asylum Records, 1982.
31. Michael Jackson, "The Girl Is Mine," *Thriller*, Epic Records, 1982.
32. Holly Near, "It's More Important To Me," Hereford Music, 1972.
33. Alice Walker, *Revolutionary Petunias* (New York: Harcourt Brace Jovanovich, 1973), p. 31.
34. Hadewijch, *Hadewijch: The Complete Works*, trans. Mother Columbia Hart O.S.B. (New York: Paulist Press, 1980), p. 186.
35. Dorothee Sölle, *Revolutionary Patience* (New York: Orbis Books, 1977), p. 51.
36. Thomas P. Fenton, ed., *Education for Justice* (Maryknoll, N.Y.: Orbis Books, 1975).
37. Ibid., p. 11.
38. Oliver Shreiner, quoted by Tillie Olsen in *Silences* (New York: Dell, 1980), p. 151.
39. Katherine Anne Porter, quoted in *Silences*, p. 165.
40. Olsen, *Silences*, p. 172.
41. Elizabeth Stuart Lyon Phelps, quoted in *Silences*, p. 208.
42. Letty (the bag lady), quoted by Sharon R. Curtin in *Nobody Ever Died of Old Age* (Boston: Little, Brown & Company, 1972), p. 90.

43. Letty Russell, *Growth in Partnership* (Philadelphia: Westminster Press, 1981), p. 26.

44. Adrienne Rich, "Claiming an Education," *On Lies, Secrets, and Silences* (New York: W. W. Norton, 1979), p. 233.

45. Rich, "Taking Women Students Seriously," *On Lies, Secrets, and Silences,* p. 233.

46. Mary Kay Thompson Tetreault, "Women in U.S. History—Beyond a Patriarchal Perspective," *Bulletin for the Council on Interracial Books for Children,* 11, No. 5, p. 10.

Chapter 4

Education for Peace: A Feminist Issue

REGINA COLL

It would be a great mistake for any one community to claim for itself the title of Peacemaker. The holy writings of every major religion extol peace and peacemaking; yet they have all waged holy wars in the name of their God. Every nation on earth proclaims itself to be a protector of the peace; yet history is a chronology of broken treaties and wars, of bombs and carnage.

True peacemakers come in all sizes and shapes, in all colors, races, and creeds. They are men and they are women. It remains for each of us to search our own tradition and discover what our contributions have been and what our responsibilities are. In this essay I share the musings of a Christian and a feminist. I leave it to others to enrich us with their traditions.

Christian feminists have two traditions which support and undergird their efforts toward peace. The first is the overwhelming evidence in the gospels that peace was a value of Jesus; the second is the somewhat hidden and forgotten history of women's involvement in peacemaking. Taken together, these two threads weave a fabric which may be used to design an education whose content is peace but also an education whose process is peace.

Christians and Peace

Peace is the promise which marks the beginning of the life of Jesus. The heavenly chorus greeted the shepherds with a song of glory to God and peace to all people of good will. Peace is also the promise which marks the end of the life of Jesus. He comforted his disciples at the last supper with the greeting of "Peace I give to you, my own peace I leave you, a peace the world cannot give, this is my gift to you" (John 14:27). After the resurrection, among the few words of Jesus which John records "Peace be to you" appears three times.

Peace is also included in the litany of blessings which is the hallmark of Jesus' teaching. Peacemakers, we are told, will be called children of God.

Peace and peacemaking were so valued by the first Christians that they would not serve in the army; such was their horror of violence that they would not even attend the popular gladiatorial combats. It was this ideal of peace which led to martyrdom for some of those first Christian pacifists. But in just three short centuries that ideal was lost, as are so many, because of political developments. When Christianity was accepted by Constantine as a state religion, it began to affect the Roman Empire, but it was also affected by it. Eventually, God and country were so identified that a man had to be Christian in order to serve in the army. We have even evolved a tradition of blessing bullets and bombs; holy wars have been waged in the name of the Prince of Peace as they have been in the name of Allah and Yahweh and Baal. We have a highly sophisticated theology of a just war and only the beginnings of a theology of peacemaking.

The peace of which Jesus spoke and which identified the early church is not a mere cessation of hostilities, nor a period of calm between armed conflicts. This peace is not an absence of war, but the presence of justice, integrity, and wholeness. It is a positive vital force. It is Shalom, reconciliation between peoples and reconciliation with God. This peace describes a world no longer hostile but harmonious; a world where justice and love reign. It is both a gift of God and the work of human hands.

Women and Peace

The indexes of most traditional history books do not list either peace or women, and this lack is a sad and dangerous distortion of human experience. Traditional history, that is, patriarchal history, has preserved for us the image of the noble wife or mother courageously sending her husband or son off to war; her pain is exceeded only by her courage. The double message, of course, is that women's suffering caused by war is deeper, more poignant, if less dramatic than men's and that, even in the face of that agony, women support war. There is another picture, however, which is only now coming into focus.

Throughout the ages women have made varied and unique contributions to the cause of peace. We read, for instance, a Greek tragedy which records the successful efforts of the women in bringing about peace. Frustrated after years of armed conflict, the women gathered behind Lysistrata and vowed not to sleep with their husbands and lovers until the war was ended. It should not come as a surprise that the warriors found a quick solution to their differences.

In our own country the first women's movement and the first peace movement grew out of the struggle against slavery. The New England Non-Resistance Society was founded in 1838 and the first women's convention was held at

Seneca Falls in 1848. The membership list of both contain many of the same names; names of women and men active in the abolition movement.

Among the most active of these was Lucretia Mott, a Quaker who understood the relationship between slavery, the oppression of women, and armed violence and who worked steadfastly against them wherever they appeared. Her argument that the principles of nonresistance ought to be applied in homes and schools as well as in public life was not too kindly received by some of the male members of the Non-Resistance Society. They did not comprehend, as did Mott, the connection between violence in the public forum and the violence which exists in homes, schools, and churches.[1]

The name of Susan B. Anthony is so closely associated with the women's movement that we have lost sight of her efforts toward peace. Long before Mahatma Gandhi and Martin Luther King, Jr., those saints of nonviolence and peace, Susan B. Anthony led small groups of women in active but nonviolent stands against oppression. In 1872, almost a half century before women were finally granted the franchise, she and sixteen other women committed an act of civil disobedience by illegally voting. At her trial and conviction, she refused to pay the fine of one hundred dollars stating, "If it please your honor, I shall never pay a dollar of your unjust penalty. . . and I shall earnestly and presistently continue to urge all women to the practical recognition of the old revolutionary maxim, that, 'Resistance to tyranny is obedience to God.' "[2] She reminds us that peacemaking has nothing to do with submission to injustice and oppression.

The litany of women peacemakers is a long one whose history has yet to be adequately celebrated. The great names in traditional history books are generals and revolutionaries, war heroes and victors. Women are conspicuous by their absence; when we look at the list of people who are honored for their efforts for peace, however, a different pattern emerges.

Still, not enough is known of these peacemakers. Who, for instance, knows the names of Bertha von Suttner, Rosika Schwimmer, or Emily Greene Balch, all Nobel Peace Prize recipients. Who knows the contributions to peace of women who distinguished themselves in other fields, women such as Elizabeth Cady Stanton and Jane Addams? Who remembers that Jeannette Rankin, U.S. Representative from Montana was the only member of Congress to vote against both the first and the second World Wars? Or that she was still active in the peace movement during the Vietnam war?[3] In our own day, who remembers the efforts of Mairead Corrigan and Betty Williams, the women who captured the imagination of the world when they managed to bring together Irish women, both Protestant and Catholic, to work for peace?

We need someone to write a history of peacemakers in order to give a fuller picture of our past. Such a history would remind us that we do have role models, we do have a history, we do have a tradition of peacemaking. Such a history would not only fill gaps, it would also set traditional history in a different context. We may have to rewrite all of our history in the light of the contribution of peacemakers.

Education and Peacemaking

But what, you may ask, is the connection between education, feminism, and peacemaking? Perhaps Virginia Woolf best answered that question a half century ago. In *Three Guineas*[4] she discusses the reasons which prompted her to contribute money to various causes. The first request she considers is from a friend who asks for a donation to a peace movement; in answering that request, she sent one guinea to each one of three different causes, explaining that each one of the three contributed to peace.

The first coin was sent to a poor and struggling women's college on the provision that it not imitate the powerful universities which inculcated not a hatred of force but the use of it, not generosity and magnanimity but anxiety to keep one's own possessions, grandeur, and power. Some might argue that universities do not foster force, possessiveness, and anxiety for power. Yet there is evidence of fear, anger, and hatred on the part of the male students and faculty which kept women from being admitted into universities or from being granted degrees, even when they had fulfilled all of the requirements. This history suggests that traditional education was not sufficient to prevent such behavior and may even have unwittingly contributed to it.

The education which Ms. Woolf proposes for women is based on two qualities which she perceived in a struggling women's college: It was poor and it was young. These two qualities could allow a college to be venturesome, to be experimental, to be created anew by each generation of students and not be weighed down with unthinking loyalty to questionable traditions.

But Virginia Woolf says it most eloquently herself:

What should be taught in the new college, the poor college? Not the arts of dominating other people; not the arts of ruling, of killing, of acquiring land and capital. . . . The poor college must teach only the arts that can be taught cheaply and be practiced by poor people, such as medicine, mathematics, music, painting, and literature. It should teach the arts of human intercourse; the art of understanding other people's lives and minds, and the little arts of talk, and of cookery, those which are allied with them. The aim of the new college, the cheap college, should not be to segrgate and specialize, but to combine. It should explore the ways in which mind and body can be made to cooperate; discover what new combinations made good wholes in human life. The teachers should be drawn from the good livers as well as from the good thinkers.[5]

Good education does not compartmentalize or set up a hierarchy that values the abstract and logical more than the material and the aesthetic. I am not suggesting here a diminution of rigorous academic investigation; what I am suggesting is an elimination of a dualistic view of the world which sets up polar relationships such as mind/body, male/female, and human/nonhuman. Because we disvalue the second partner in each of these pairs, our exaltation of the first is distorted. Setting up adversarial relationships between mind and body gives rise to a kind of gnostic hatred of the body. More than that, and not so evident, it leads to a development of the mind which is not integrated nor whole. We simply do not know what the human mind is capable of because we have learned to think of it as separate from the body.

We also do not know what men are really capable of because we have been so busy defining them in opposition to women. What might human beings accomplish if they did not identify themselves against nature, superior to the rest of creation, ready to subdue it, called to lord over it?

Perhaps the thing that will finally convert some men to a feminist mind-set will be the realization that their minds have not been fully developed because of the negative ideas we have about the body; that men do not know what they are capable of becoming because so-called feminine qualities are denigrated; that men and women do not really appreciate what it means to be human because we have lost sight of our relationship to the whole of creation.

The Peaceable Classroom

We might ask what a classroom would be like when peace is a value. First, the domination-subordination relationship between teacher and student is at a minimum in such a setting. Of course, as an adult and as a professional, the educator has a responsibility for providing an atmosphere in which learning may take place. But the relationship resembles what Jean Baker Miller refers to as temporary dependence. Temporary dependence is, as its name implies, a relationship which exists for a period of time and which ordinarily exists for the benefit of the weaker partner in the relationship. Parents, counselors, and doctors are in a position of temporary domination over children, clients, and patients. The aim of the relationship is to end the inequality and not to keep people in a position of subordination and dependence. Thus, parents strive to raise independent adults, counselors strive to avoid any transfer of dependency to them, and doctors work to bring patients to full health.[6]

When schools do not operate to eliminate dependence, they may be guilty of causing "pedogenic illnesses," that is, learning disabilities caused by teachers in much the same way that doctors cause iatrogenic illnesses. But, "even doctors, in their heyday as godlike paragons, have never wielded the authority of a single classroom teacher, who can purvey prizes, failure, love, humiliation, and information to great numbers of relatively powerless vulnerable young people."[7] Children who come to school filled with excitement and a spirit of creativity and adventure often find enough discouragement and domination to squelch that spirit and foster a numb uncritical compliance.

There is no place in a peaceable classroom for the use of either physical, emotional, or psychological violence. Students may behave well in such a setting; order may be maintained and discipline instilled. But it is a discipline from without, not a self-discipline which would strengthen character. Education of this kind develops obedient, amoral adults who are incapable of saying no to authority. The now famous experiments of Stanley Milgram are frightening reminders of the danger of unthinking obedience. Milgram ordered his subjects to administer what they believe to be ever increasing dosages of electricity to another person. In reality, there was no electricity flowing and the "victim" only pretended to be in pain. Sixty-five percent of the people involved obeyed the order to increase the shock in spite of terrible cries of anguish. The urge to conform, to submit to authority, to obey was so strong that the subjects were willing to inflict what they believed to be potentially dangerous shocks when ordered to do so. A further troubling conclusion of these experiments is that people who identified themselves as belonging to some religion were more docile and obedient and were more willing to inflict greater electrical impulses than people who claimed no religious affiliation.

Dorothee Sölle in her challenging work, *Beyond Mere Obedience*,[8] calls for a radical rethinking of obedience as a Christian virtue. Writing in the aftermath of Nazi Germany and in the light of many Christians' cooperation with Hitler, Sölle writes:

> Why did Jesus not normatively determine what God's will is instead of encouraging us to discover this will in each given situation? . . . is this God of exclusive obedience really the God of Jesus Christ?[9]

We need fewer conformists, more independent adults who do not excuse themselves from responsibility because someone in authority issues an order.

Another characteristic of a peaceable classroom is the

minimizing of competition and the maximizing of cooperation. The "We're number one" syndrome, whether in sports, academic achievement, or national identity often leads people to judge their own worth, progress, and success by their ability to beat someone else. They learn that competition is the name of the game, that happiness and even one's self-image depend on being better than others. Teachers in peace-loving classrooms avoid games and contests in which one person wins and everyone else loses; they might avoid motivating students by pitting them against one another. They certainly would not set up teams of boys-against-girls. But, you might argue, it works—there are students who work best when they are competing.

And you are absolutely right.

What we forget is that competition is learned behavior and every time we depend on it we are reinforcing the lesson that life is about beating other people. Students often learn more than we intend to teach.

If students learn to work together in groups; if they learn from one another (not merely a bright student tutoring a slower one); if student's groups prepare projects and panels for the benefit of the whole class and not in order to compete for the best grades; if students take team tests, working together toward a team grade, then perhaps they will learn that cooperation rather than competition is a viable way of learning and of living.

We can't argue that competition, violence, or war are part of human nature since the discovery of the gentle Tassaday tribe. The Tassaday do not even have a word for war. War is not part of their vocabulary because it is not part of their lives. Someone in their distant past must have taught them to depend on one another rather than compete. Our students need that lesson, too. They can learn that interdependence and cooperation will make for a better and more peaceful classroom, home, school, and world.

A third important characteristic of a peaceable classroom is that it has a structure for conflict resolution. It would be naive to presume that a teacher who strives to eliminate domination and competition would also be able to eliminate disruption. Original sin is too much with us for that.

Very often people react in a violent way to conflict because they are unprepared for it—they are taken off guard. Decisions are then made in the heat of passion, anger, or frustration. What is needed is a system for conflict resolution that is understood and preferably determined by all. Even the youngest of children are capable of some beginnings of corporate decision making. They can help draw up the rules, help make decisions that affect them and determine how infractions will be handled. Discussions about justice and compassion tempering justice may be helpful here but the most beneficial part is the actual experience.

The experience of enacting laws, of revising them and of sometimes recalling them can teach more about the nature, benefits, and shortcomings of living by law than can any lecture or discussion. We might even suggest that in helping to determine the sanctions for classroom "crimes" students may be brought to evaluate the merits of punishment for punishment sake and correction for the sake of rehabilitation. We might go so far as to hope that when enough students change their ideas on punishment, they may be able to effect a change in the American attitude toward the violence that is capital punishment. Eventually, we may even hope that the United States will remove itself from the dubious distinction it shares with only three other technologically developed nations in permitting capital punishment. Then only Japan, South Africa, and Russia would remain.

But conflict resolution is not primarily about punishment. It is concerned with the art of negotiation and compromise. Disagreements are often settled violently because the stronger person or group can subdue the weaker and claim victory. There is little correspondence between justice and peace and the solution of the problem. Conflict resolution in practice can give students the tools with which to handle future difficulties. Students, young and old alike, need to learn how to listen, really listen, to other people's opinions; they need to learn not to reject a person who disagrees with them. They need to learn that in some situations, if each adversary gives in a little, a compromise can be made that both parties can live with.

These suggestions are meant to begin a discussion on education for peace; they share the fundamental concepts of other suggestions in this area: "That children should learn to live in harmony with themselves and their peers so they will enter the adult world with the sense that reconciliation, instead of war, is the road to peace."[10]

Two Closing Remarks

The first of my closing remarks is by way of explaining why I chose to speak of education in terms of school. I believe that everything that I said is applicable in non-school settings and that the transfer is obvious. But more than that, most of what is being written in the area of peace and justice is concerned with adult education. Yet unless we begin to teach young people in a manner that is both peaceful and just we will soon have another generation in need of basic peace and justice education.

The second remark has to do with the values discussed as appropriate for a peaceable classroom. Feminist readers will recognize them as basic values of the feminist movement. I did not present them as such in order to avoid the kind of pitfall we fall into when we speak of Christian charity as if people who are not Christian are not charitable or as if charity which is Christian is more valuable than Jewish or Moslem charity. The qualities which I proposed are feminist values, but they are also human values. Feminism may be presenting these qualities in a new way, but it has not invented them. Let us learn to be happy that feminist values are embraced even if feminism is still beyond acceptance.

The Content of a Course on Education for Peace

I have said nothing about what courses on peace might look like. The reason for this is that there are already excellent curriculum guides, printed matter and audiovisuals available. My best contribution here may be to suggest some of the materials on the subject.

First and foremost, teachers and others interested in learning about peace may wish to join Educators for Social Responsibility, 639 Massachusetts Avenue, Cambridge, MA 20139. The dues are $10.00. They have a very fine listing of materials available through their office.

Other suggestions follow, but if the listing does not include an office in your area, you can call your religious affiliation judicatory center and ask for the office for peace and justice. They are eager to be of assistance and if your religious center does not already have such an office established, your call may serve as a catalyst.

Suggestions for Children

UNICEF Peace Education Kit ($2.00)
U.S. Committee for UNICEF
331 East 38rd Street
New York NY 10016

Peacemaking Activities for Children ($3.00 plus $2.00 handling)
Brethren House
6301 56th Avenue, North
St. Petersburg FL 33709

Peacing it Together ($9.95 plus $1.50 handling)
17095 Southwest Eldorado Drive
Tigard OR 97223

Sadako and the Thousand Paper Cranes (slides)
Institute for Peace and Justice
4144 Lindell #400
St. Louis MO 63108

For Adolescents

Blessed are the Peacemakers ($6.50 plus $.75 handling)
Pax Center
345 East 9 Street
Erie PA 16503

Under the Mushroom Cloud (slides: rental $5.00)
Nuclear War Graphics Project
100 Nevada Street
Northfield MN 55074

Gods of Metal (film: rental $25.00)
Maryknoll
Maryknoll NY 10545

Violence, U.S.A.: What Kind of People Are We?
Fellowship of Reconciliation
Box 271
Nyack NY 10960

For Adults, Parents, Teachers, and Others

Parenting for Peace and Justice ($4.95)
Orbis Books
Maryknoll NY 10545

A Checklist of Nuclear Books, March 26, 1982
Publishers Weekly
1190 Avenue of Americas
New York NY 10036

Ground Zero Bibliography (Up to 3 copies free)
Ground Zero
806 15th Street, NW
Washington DC 20005

NOTES

1. See for instance, Margaret H. Bacon, "Non-Violence and Women,"
   "The Pioneers," in *Reweaving the Web of Life: Feminism and Non-Violence*, ed. Pam McAllister (Philadelphia: New Society Publishers, 1982), pp. 78-84.
2. See Josephine Rubin, "Women and Peace," *The Whole Earth Papers* 1, No. 6 (Spring, 1978).
3. For more on Jeannette Rankin see Hannah Josephson, *Jeannette Rankin* (Indianapolis: Bobbs Merrill, 1974).
4. Virginia Woolf, *Three Guineas* (New York: Harcourt Brace Jovanovich, 1966).
5. Ibid., p. 34.
6. Jean Baker Miller, *Toward a New Psychology of Women* (Boston: Beacon Press, 1976), pp. 3-5.
7. Marilyn Ferguson, *The Aquarian Conspiracy* (Boston: Houghton Mifflin, 1980), p. 283.
8. Dorothee Sölle, *Beyond Mere Obedience*, trans. Lawrence W. Denef (New York: Pilgrim Press, 1982).
9. Ibid., p. 22.
10. Gordon Oliver, "Teaching Peace to Our Children," *National Catholic Reporter*, December 12, 1982, p. 13.

Chapter 5

The Role of Religious Education in Preventing Sexual and Domestic Violence

JANET TANAKA

Introduction

"The family must be preserved!" The cry comes from Unitarians on the left and Mormons on the right, echoed by every Christian denomination in between—and not only from the Christians. From Jews, Moslems, Hindus, Buddhists, and Baha'is comes the plea: Save the family!

And yet it is within the family that one out of every two women is battered and that half of all sexual abuse of children occurs.[1] A shockingly high number of the reported cases of child abuse occur in families that claim to be Christian. Shelters for battered women fill with victims whose bodies and lives have been shattered by brutal husbands, fathers, and boyfriends. It is hard to believe that there are Christians beseeching Congress and legislatures not to appropriate money for such shelters, on the grounds that by so doing they are "destroying the family." Laws that affirm the rights to which women are entitled by their humanness, if not the Constitution, are opposed on the grounds that such rights are dangerous to the stability of the family and the home.

If human dignity, rescue from cruelty, healing and justice are the enemies of the family, then it is time to ask whether an institution that can be maintained only through the physical, mental, and spiritual destruction of human beings is *worth* saving.

Perhaps it is time for a Good Samaritan to happen along. We have, in recent times, lost the original meaning of Jesus' parable; that the Good Samaritan was not a friend, but an enemy who helped when the friends had all turned away for fear of getting involved. Perhaps these "enemies" of the family, these social workers and do-gooders, are the Samaritans who will finally bind up the family's wounds.

They cannot do it, however, without the involvement of religion. Just as religion has been a part of the problem, so also it must be vital part of the solution. The family is a God-founded institution. It has existed in one form or another since the beginning of human society. It is the "little church," the reflection of God's interaction with his people. From the earliest religious expressions of thanksgiving and sacrifice for fertility of harvest and harvester, down through the ages the relationship of human beings to their deity(ies) has often been one of family. Such images as "Mother Earth and Father Sky," the "Bride of Christ," and the "Children of Israel," are commonly found in religious word and thought.

The God who loves us made us male and female and gave us family. He gave us Love.

What went wrong?

The purpose of this paper is to show, first, the misinterpretations of Holy Scripture that have condoned sexual abuse and violence against women and children. These are errors that religious education programs have a duty to address and correct, through explanations such as the ones used here. Programs of religious education can and must be used to replace the roadblocks of ignorance with the bridges of understanding. After all, is that not the purpose of *all* education? Part III will offer some suggestions as to specific types of programs and/or techniques that can be used. The fourth section will focus briefly on the pioneering religious organization in this specific field; the Center for the Prevention of Sexual and Domestic Violence.

I. Religion as a Part of the Problem

It is easy to see how a person's religion can be a resource to strengthen families. However, any poorly understood religious belief in the hands and hearts of people experiencing stresses and tensions, people who have a poor self-image, people who are fearful, can become not only a roadblock to family healing but can itself become a tool for inflicting hurt. In our religious communities we tell ourselves: "These things don't happen here. Our people are good people." Statistics and casebooks, however, tell another story.

It is a tragic fact that much domestic violence and sexual abuse is reinforced by so-called "religious" teachings that in most cases are misunderstandings, misinterpretations, and (sometimes) deliberate perversions of the teachings of the prophets of God. The original God-given teachings have been altered or displaced by human fears, human greed, human conceit, human stubbornness, human selfishness, and all those contrary traits that make up/stem from original sin.

For example: Moses' commandment to honor thy father and mother has been perverted to "children have no rights." The Old Testament prophets' teachings on humility have been twisted to "I am worthless." Jesus' example of obedience to his mission and his acceptance of the bitter cup of crucifixion have somehow become "suffering is good for the soul, and happiness and fun are tools of the devil." Mohammad's bold actions in raising women from no-status-at-all, commanding their protection, and giving them the rights to their own property has been perverted back to what—in our modern society—amounts to no-status-at-all.

Certainly St. Paul never intended his words to mean nonpersonhood for women. Some forget that he also wrote: "Husbands love your wives as Christ loved the church." Nowhere is it written that Christ ever slammed the church up against the wall because the dinner was cold or the beer warm.

Using Scripture to justify, or even to unconsciously aid and abet, violence against women and children is not an exclusively Christian sin. Jews, Moslems, and Buddhists are also guilty. Even the Baha'i faith, which teaches a creed of nonviolence and spells out in no uncertain terms the equality of the sexes, has to deal with misinterpretations that result in violent or potentially abusive situations going uncorrected.

Abuse of Wives

Clearly the Old Testament books mirrored the values of the culture in which they were written, but they were not intended to show contempt for women. Israelite women were never degraded as they were in the religions surrounding them. Prostitution was not a form of Hebrew religious practice, nor was the sacrificing of virgins or infants. Men were masters of their homes (Genesis 3:16), but children were required by Mosaic law to give their mothers and fathers equal respect (Exodus 20:12, 21:17, and Leviticus 19:3). It can be inferred that men must also have respected their wives, else the children would not have done so.

The Rev. Marie Fortune[2] cites seven Old Testament sources on sexual violence: Joseph and Potiphar's wife (Genesis 39:11-30), Susanna and the Elders (Daniel 13 and the Apocrypha), the Levite and the Concubine (Judges 19:11-30), the rape of Dinah (Genesis 34), the rape of Tamar (2 Samuel 13), and laws found in Deuteronomy 22:23-29 and Leviticus 18:6-18. To these could be added Queen Vashti (Esther 1:10-20), who was punished because she refused to be paraded before a roomful of her husband's drunken friends.

Potiphar's wife is used as an example of false accusation of rape. Susanna is the only raped woman who is vindicated and treated with sympathy, but she had to be rescued by Daniel because, as a woman, she was not allowed to speak in her own defense. The concubine, however, is treated as a piece of disposable merchandise. The assaults on Dinah and Tamar are regarded as assaults, not on their own human dignity, but on the value of another's property. Deuteronomy and Leviticus also regard women as property and assaults on them as crimes against the men to whom they "belong."

Yet, it must be said that Deuteronomy 5, which places the coveting of a wife above the coveting of property—thus separating her from mere chattels—is an improvement over Exodus 20, which lumps them all together.

It was the rabbinic traditions that evolved in the centuries following the revelations that misinterpreted or failed to reinterpret the teachings, perpetuating the untruths and half-truths which portrayed women as nonpersons. Rabbi Sally Priesand[3] cites the Talmud and the legend of Lilith as other sources of antifemale beliefs and practices. Biblical scholarship, in tracing the source documents for the Old Testament, has revealed the falsity of the Lilith myth, which for centuries was cited to keep Jewish women in their place. We know now that the two creation stories in Genesis were from two different sources or narratives, rather than one continuous story, as once was thought. The first pictures man and woman as being equally created. In the second, woman is made from man's rib. For centuries these were erroneously interpreted as being all one narrative, telling how Adam's first wife—traditionally given the name of Lilith—considered herself Adam's equal and refused to be bossed around by him. Therefore, she was removed from the picture, and Eve—the woman of the second story—was made to be properly submissive. Tradition and folklore have ingrained into Jewish women the "lesson" that independence and uppityness are punishable offenses.

While many of the sayings of the Talmud downgrade women's intelligence, integrity, and dignity, still others extol women for their understanding and compassion. Men are cautioned not to hurt their wives' feelings. They are told that domestic peace is assured the man who loves his wife as himself and honors her more than himself. Nowhere in Jewish law is wife-beating condoned, and divorce has always been an option, says Rabbi Priesand, for the Jewish woman who is abused. Taken as a whole, women got a far better deal under those laws than in most countries governed by the Christian church.

Turning to the New Testament, there is a striking contrast between the way in which Jesus treated women and the way some of his followers behave. Sarah Perkins, in *The Woman's Bible*,[4] points out that, while Christ delivered several stinging rebukes to men—including his own disciples—there is no record of his speaking harshly to a woman. He chided some, but never told them off as he did men. That he regarded women as full human beings is made obvious in the 11th chapter of Luke, where a well-meaning woman praises Jesus' mother for having borne and suckled him. Many women, even today, are raised to think of themselves only as wives and mothers. But Jesus admonishes the woman who, without thinking, has defined her sex as wombs and breasts. "Rather," he says, "blessed are they that hear the word of God and keep it." Blessedness has been redefined in a nonsexual way. It is open to everyone on an equal basis and not through one's relationship to another.

This teaching stands in direct and stunning contradiction to those contemporary Christian writers who insist that a woman can only exist in relation to her husband, a teaching which in itself is a gross form of mental and emotional abuse, for it robs a woman of her dignity and individual worth as a child of God.

The most telling example of Jesus' respect for women is that he chose a woman to whom to announce his resurrection message. Whether or not one's religious creed accepts the literal bodily resurrection is immaterial. The gospel says that it was to a woman that the truth of victory over physical and spiritual death was announced, and a woman was chosen to bring the message to the other followers. When we recall that women were not acceptable witnesses in courts of law in those times, how delightful it is to see that God chooses women to proclaim Truth when men will not accept their word as to fact!

What has this to do with domestic and sexual violence? Having seen the regard in which Jesus held women, it is difficult to understand how many Christians could have interpreted Paul to have said the exact opposite. While the first half of Paul's message: "Wives, obey your husbands as you would the Lord," always seems to get through, somehow the second half: "Husbands, love your wives as Christ loved the church," seems almost always to disappear into limbo. "Christ/husband" sacrificed and suffered and died for his "church/wife." Why is it that so many Christian wives are told to sacrifice, suffer, and die—spiritually, intellectually, and sometimes even physically—for their husbands? There are a lot of un-Christlike husbands out there destroying their "churches." Sadly, they are being cheered on by dozens of books telling wives to commit suicide by disowning their emotions, thoughts, talents, and selves and to commit idolatry by worshiping their husbands!

Moses, Christ, and St. Paul all made it clear that no human being is ever to be worshiped. All human beings are fallible. All need correcting. All can do wrong. No one, save God and the holy prophets and messengers chosen to represent the deity on earth, has the right to demand universal, absolute, unquestioning obedience. Kings, presidents, husbands, and parents have no such right. There is a time for obedience and a time for considering disobedience. The Nuremberg trials and My Lai have made "I was only following orders" no longer acceptable in a moral world.

There is another facet of biblical teaching that has indirectly contributed to the sufferings of women involved in domestic or sexual violence: that of God as a righteous judge who gives people what they deserve while they are still on earth. The victim of evil is still often seen as evil, for the Scriptures say that "it shall be well" with the righteous and "it shall be ill" for the wicked (Isaiah 3:10-11). There is little doubt that God does judge, but as it is demonstrated so clearly in the book of Job, the righteous also suffer through no fault of their own. Nevertheless, it is from this equation of earthly suffering with punishment that we get some of the blame-the-victim syndrome. Suffering is also touted as the sure way into heaven, whence we get the doctrines of asceticism. Suffering is our purifier. (God loves us so much he makes us miserable!?)

Where suffering is concerned, we have somehow allowed

ourselves to believe that God, who is Love, sits upon a throne pulling the wings off us human flies to see how we squirm. Why should Love deliberately and calculatedly send pain, misery, and cruelty upon such greatly loved children? The message of the Incarnation is that God took on the human form and died because of love for us; why then inflict torture on that creation to see how much it could take? Jesus pointed out that God is far kinder than the loving human fathers (or parents) who give their children bread instead of stones (Matthew 7:9).

The idea that God has given a woman or man an abusive spouse to "test" or "strengthen" her/him is nothing short of barbaric. It is impossible to gain such an idea from the gospels. We forget that free will and sin entered the world at the same time. Neither Moses nor Christ excused evil. They bade their followers to cast it out of themselves. God is not responsible for our sins and the sins of others. We are and they are. God gives us strength to make it come out all right. God allows us to be tested by earthly suffering rather than swooping down in a golden helicopter and rescuing us, because we can grow by passing the test. God also knows that some will fail—at least by earthly standards, and for these precious ones there is compassion.

Millions of words have been written about suffering, some wise and others not only foolish but dangerous. It is important for the women who is being abused to understand that she is not being punished, she is not being tested. She is being abused by a man who is committing a sin against another child of God and against the God who created them both. Her suffering is not making either one of them any better or holier persons.

Western criticism of the Islamic world frequently overlooks the fact that the Quran gave women rights and protections previously unknown among the barbaric tribes of

Arabia. Before Mohammad, girls and young women were often buried alive or beaten to death. A woman with no man to support her was often left to starve or become a prostitute. Mohammad explicitly forbade such treatment. He gave laws to protect woman's dignity and modesty. One of the purposes of allowing multiple wives was to assure every woman and girl a husband to care for and protect her. Under Islam, women were given the rights of inheritance and property ownership in this life and assurance of paradise in the next. But, as with the earlier teachings of Paul, the real meanings of these laws were beyond the grasp of many of Mohammad's followers.

Sexual Violence

Historical Christianity has little about which to congratulate itself where violence and sexual abuse are concerned. The prevailing attitude was well summed up in the remarks of a nineteenth-century clergyman: "My Bible commands the subjection of women forever."[5]

The Christian church further incited violence against women when it declared some of them to be witches. It was the church that described women as "evil, subject to carnal lust, weak, impressionable, defective, impulsive, and liars by nature,"[6] and it was the church that decided virginity was more important than existence. The latter idea stems, of course, from the "damaged goods" thinking which relegated women to the status of property rather than persons.

Much of the church's thinking on sexual violence has been muddled by the confusion between sexual violence and sexual activity. They focus on the sexual component rather than the violence. This leads to the infamous blame-the-victim line of thinking. A woman who has been sexually assaulted "must have" done something to cause it—she must have tempted him. This kind of thinking leads to an interesting contradiction. On one hand, it is the woman who is supposed to be "weak, impulsive, and lustful." Yet, it is the poor weak, impulsive, lustful male who cannot control his raging passions at the glimpse of cleavage or a leg! People who use this excuse apparently do not realize that they are reducing their fathers, brothers, and sons to a sub-human level; denying that males are creatures made in the image and likeness of God and implying instead that they are lacking in any kind of self-control or human decency—animals ruled entirely by chance passions, unfit to be let loose on the streets, and hardly to be trusted to run the business, factories, and governments of the world! Yet, are these not the "reasons" that have been used to rule women as unfit to run things?

Abuse of Children

The teachings of both Old and New Testaments regarding the obedience children owe their parents are frequently used to justify child abuse. "Spare the rod . . ." is interpreted to mean that children must be physically beaten. When combined with the doctrine of original sin the result is often: Children are born evil and must be beaten to save their souls. At the very least, the result is a belief that children will "go to the devil" if not punished frequently and harshly. Yet, Ephesians 6:4 also cautions fathers not to provoke their children's anger! And is the "rod" a physical punishment or does the word refer to the rod used by the shepherd to protect his sheep (Psalm 23:4), the metaphorical rod of guidance and instruction?

The commandment to honor parents is reinforced in Ephesians 6:1-3. This teaching became "proof" that children have no rights to their own bodies, thoughts, or feelings. Over and over again judges and social workers in cases of child abuse hear this commandment quoted to justify the behavior of the defendants. The victims, too, have heard all these teachings. They have been told in Sunday School (or Sabbath School or Temple or CCD) that they must *always* obey parents, no matter what they demand. No one, until very recently, has told the children that this does not include sexual abuse and incest.

II. Roadblocks

It would be wonderful to relegate the old mistakes to history, but we have not reached that point. There are several more that need to be mentioned, for they continue to create a climate for all kinds of abuse against women and children. They are (a) God is male and only males are godlike; (b) divorce breaks up homes and therefore should not be permitted; (c) we must have nonviolence at any price; (d) forgiveness covers all; (e) the self is evil; (f) we must say only good things about people—no matter how badly they have acted.

a. Nature of God

Although the Holy Scriptures tell us repeatedly that God is a Spirit whose ways are higher than ours, yet we persist in making the assumption that God is somehow a greatly magnified male human being (probably white and Anglo) from the planet earth. Although this is the worst blasphemy, we still think and behave as if it were so. A spirit has no body, for a body must exist in space and time and God transcends both. God is sovereign of all the universe—a universe that most likely contains innumerable other intelligent spiritual beings, few if any of whom may resemble *terran homo sapiens,* male *or* female, but who are also made in the image and likeness of the Creator.

Yet, in what better way could God show us the attributes of strength and tenderness, justice and compassion, wisdom, understanding, and guidance than as a father. Not a fallible human father. Not a domineering, cruel, incestuous father, but the ultimate in father-ness. While God is the ideal father to whom all human fathers must look for a model, God is also the ideal mother. But in the light of many centuries of worship of female deities—worship which had become corrupt and degraded—the image of mother seems inappropriate for the part of the world where "he" revealed "himself" at the time. As the sun of reality dawns upon the world, we are better able to see and comprehend the all-inclusiveness of God's nature; thus the efforts by many Christian scholars to revise the language of the Scriptures to better reflect that nature. The doctrine of the Holy Trinity attempts to explain the many facets of God's being. He is "Father"   but Genesis says that God made the human race *both* male and female in "his" image. God is "son," but the authors of the New Testament refer to Christ's human nature as *anthropos* (human) and not *aner* (male). God is Spirit, but "the Holy Spirit" is frequently referred to as the feminine component of the Trinity, especially in Eastern-rite churches. Certainly many of the images used in world religions to signify the Holy Spirit are feminine in nature, e.g. the dove, the "Maid of Heaven," and "still small voice."

When the term "father" describes an earthly father who is loving, kind, and protective, God is seen in that light. However, when human fathers commit crimes against their children and their children's mothers, they may easily poison their children's minds and souls against the concept of "father" and ultimately God.

Hearkening back to the writers who teach women to

submit to their husband's authority, we face the question of what happens to the man who is made a god. What happens to the psyche of a human being who is given absolute power over others? Does he become more loving, more unselfish, more considerate and sensitive to the needs of his wife and children? "Power tends to corrupt and absolute power corrupts absolutely" is not a maxim for government alone. What is more, a human being who gives away her own power in such a submissive relationship runs the risk of creating a very unscriptural monster! Does a spoiled child whose every whim is obeyed, whose tantrums are law, become lovely and loving? Neither does a spoiled adult. For those who believe in Original Sin and the ease by which our fallen natures can be led astray, what excuse is there for contributing to the spiritual downfall of the husband one has promised before God to love and honor?

It is Christ who washed the feet of the loved ones, not the other way around. If a husband loves his wife as Christ loves the church, then he must heed Jesus' words that the one who wishes to be the greatest must be the servant of all. It is clear from the gospels that the highest station of any Christian is to be the servant of the servants of God. We are all called to the greatness of servitude. In the Pauline concept of the ideal Christian marriage, husband and wife lovingly serve each other, sacrificing for each other, pleasing each other, honoring each other. The ideal means never nagging, belittling, depriving, dominating, manipulating, abusing, raping, or hitting each other. First Corinthians 13 is for all.

b. Divorce

Divorce does not break up homes. It is, rather, a sign that the covenant between husband and wife is already broken. The insistence on keeping the family together at all costs has often had a high cost indeed, especially where there is any kind of physical or sexual abuse. Divorce is the symptom of the broken family and not the cause. We will do better to find the cause of the symptoms and to treat the disease rather than condemn people who are exhibiting signs of marital illness. Making divorce more difficult will only worsen the ailment and add to the toll of battered bodies, minds, and souls. Yet, we have those in the Christian (and other) communities who think they can solve the problems of broken homes by tightening the legal system.

c. Nonviolence

One of the best summary interpretations of Jesus' teaching on self-defense and nonviolence comes from the writings of 'Abd'l-Baha'.[7]

> Thus when Christ said: "Whosoever shall smite thee on the right cheek, turn to him the left one also," it was for the purpose of teaching men not to take personal revenge. He did not mean that, if a wolf should fall upon a flock of sheep and wish to destroy it, the wolf should be encouraged to do so. No, if Christ had known that a wolf had entered the fold and was about to destroy the sheep, most certainly he would have prevented it.

To quote Marie Fortune: "To the extent that Christian teaching prevents women from even considering self-protection seriously, it does us a disservice."[8] Jesus did not intend that human beings, made in the image of God, be victimized and abused. Furthermore this only contributes to the continued sinfulness of the sinner and makes us an accomplice in the sin! Our bodies are temples of the Holy Spirit, we are told. How could God command us to allow these temples to be desecrated? Nonviolence also tends to have a double standard in preaching and practice. The male preacher who tells a woman she has no right to use violence to defend herself from an abuser may on the next Sunday defend the building and use of nuclear weapons!

d. Forgiveness

A related gospel teaching that often becomes a problem through misunderstanding is that of forgiveness. To forgive an abuser is not to excuse him or her. The God of compassion and mercy is also a God of justice. Justice is not served when an abuser goes free to abuse again. Christ forgave and then told the sinners to go but to sin no more. It is *not* okay to go on abusing, and *it is a sin against justice to let oneself* or *someone else be abused.*

Yet Jesus knew how very difficult it is for us contrary humans to change our way. Paul bewailed the fact that he could not seem to do the good he willed nor refrain from doing the evil he did not want (Romans 7:19). So, when the sinner is sincerely trying to change we must forgive "seventy times seven" and give the person a chance. However, forgiving doesn't mean that the abuser stops going to therapy or that the abused has to live with the abuser before he/she is straightened out. No reading of the Bible or any other holy book can seriously be interpreted to mean that we close our eyes to evil and allow the wolf to gobble up the sheep. The Catholic who goes to confession knows (or should know) that absolution requires a firm purpose of amendment.

Forgiving also means letting go of a painful experience. It means not continuing to say, "If only I had/hadn't . . ." It means picking up the pieces and going on with your own life.

e. Love of Self

The word "ego" causes so much confusion that it should be stricken from psychology and religion alike. Originally a value-neutral word meaning the self-image, it has come to mean in pop psychology (and unfortunately in religion) selfishness or self-centeredness. Thus, while behavioral scientists are telling us that every person needs a healthy ego, i.e., self-image, the evangelists are telling us to stamp out our evil egos. No wonder Christians and Jews and Baha'is are confused! No wonder we begin to equate humility with self-hatred and self-assurance with sin.

This kind of thing may come from some television evangelists, but it doesn't come from Jesus. We are to love ourselves and everyone else as God loves us and for the sake of God. Yes, we are all sinners, and yes, God loves us anyway.

How did Jesus tell us to love our neighbor (which the parable makes clear is everybody), but in the way that we love *ourselves?* If I hate myself, how can I love my neighbor? And if my neighbor hates himself, how can he love me?

The abuser virtually always has a negative self-image. People who love themselves do not have to beat other people either figuratively or literally. Women, especially, are told that they must never think of themselves, that everyone else counts but them. This is not Christian/Jewish/Moslem/Baha'i selflessness or humility. It leads to repressed anger, hostility, depression, self-victimization, and child abuse. Who are we to devalue what God loves? Mothers must learn to "take care of number one," because if number one becomes ill—whether physically, mentally, or spiritually—who is going to be able to take care of numbers two, three, and four?

f. Speaking of Others

"If you can't say something good about somebody don't say anything at all." It may *not be good* to say that dear old Uncle Joe is a child molester, *but it had better be said!* One of the saddest traps that sincere, loving people fall into is that of teaching their children not to say disparaging things about people. Of course fault-finding, backbiting, and scandal *are* evil in themselves and should be stamped out. They are spiteful and malicious. But there is a time for being kind and there is a time and a place for being just. The problem is that small children, who are at the greatest risk from sex offenders and abusive adults, are also too young to tell the difference between tale-bearing and reporting their fears.

We must encourage our children to be open and frank with us about people who behave in a manner that makes them uncomfortable. To turn a child off with the arbitrary rule that "we only listen to good things about people" is to place that child in great danger. Some people need to have evil spoken of them because they are people who do evil, and we must protect ourselves and our children from them. It is a jungle out there; we cannot let our desire for perfection leave our precious little ones defenseless before the onslaught of the alligators!

Teaching our children is the first step, for the home is where all religious education begins.

III. Religious Education as a Part of the Solution

The need for religious education has been shown. That education must include spiritual values—love, trust, unselfishness, compassion, respect, and reverence for God and all creation—and it must include intellectual food, such as Scripture study directed by well-trained teachers who know the history of that Scripture. It is not enough to be able to use audio-visuals or to have memorized the words. Teachers must have learned what the words mean and be able to convey that meaning in a way that makes sense to those they are instructing. Most important, they must have accepted the Word into their own hearts and minds, minds that are not afraid to question premises that don't square with the spirit in which the Scriptures were revealed. Like the blind men studying the elephant, we humans tend to take passages out of context and so miss the reality of the beast.

If serious secular literature requires study and intellectual self-discipline for understanding, how much more important that we approach Holy Scripture as carefully trained, well-disciplined students. Of course God's Word must be approached prayerfully, but with rational faculties alert and aware. We must be careful not to absolutize the culture in which the books were written, for the prophets of God bring two kinds of truth. The first is the eternal, unchanging law of God, exemplified in the Ten Commandments and the Golden Rule. Other laws, while still ordained by God, are intended for the times in which they were written. They are to correct practices of the prevailing culture that prevent the living out of the will of God in that day.

Furthermore, because the teachings were followed, the cultures eventually changed and grew nearer to what was sought by the writers. It makes no more moral sense to continue patriarchy and religious warfare than it does to continue slavery—but all these were present in biblical and Quranic times.

Religious interpretations leading to domestic and sexual abuse can only be corrected by a religious education that deals with the points discussed in Part I. The meat of that education—the ideas needing correction, clarification, re-interpretation and replacement—have already been stated. It is the *how* that remains to be considered. There are four areas in which such education must be carried out, regardless of the particular religion involved: in the home, the religious school, the religious community (church), and the society at large.

The Family

As different as their other ideas may be, all enduring religions agree on the family as the basic unit of society and the cradle of the individual's religious faith. They agree that God is the creator of humankind (although religions such as Buddhism are not based on a personal God), that we are male and female and that families are a part of the divine plan. Sexuality is the gift given to make this union possible, and it should be used within marriage with reverence and joy. Marriage calls for a lifelong commitment in which each partner helps the other develop to his or her fullest capacity, even though different religions and cultures may see various means for that development and differ as to what that capacity may be. They all affirm that children are a blessed trust from God and that parenthood is an honorable vocation.

The problem is that liberal and conservative religious teachers alike have gone too far to their respective sides of the road and fallen into attitudes and practices that are detrimental to the family, both as an institution and as individual households. Both need to be reawakened and reeducated to the needs and purposes of the family.

The most basic spiritual lesson taught in the family is that of trust. Trust begins in infancy. "Faith" is a larger kind of trust. Without trust, love is scarcely possible. Children develop trust in themselves, in others, and in God through living with parents who trust themselves, others, and God. The religious community needs to guide and strengthen the sense of trust and faith of its members, so that they can instill it in their children. When a child's trust has been shattered through violence or sexual abuse, the community of faith has a duty to intervene in the name of God and bring about the healing process.

A child who is not healed stands a strong chance of becoming an abusive parent. Many researchers have found that a majority of men in anger-control therapy have been physically abused as children or witnessed violence between their parents. The same seems to hold true in many cases for women who were battered as children.

Children who are not allowed to express normal strong emotions, who are forced to grow up too fast, who have learned that trust is usually betrayed, who have learned that it is all right to hit people when angry or dissatisfied with them, that others are to be blamed when things go wrong, that the self is evil and self-worth is bad—all these children frequently grow up to abuse their own children emotionally and spiritually and/or physically.

It is not entirely true that "the family that prays together stays together." Misunderstandings and misinterpretation of religious teachings have often led to family beliefs and practices which are so harmful that some families become spiritually, emotionally, and even physically torn apart. The duty of religious leaders and teachers, then, is to help the families in their charge to a healthy spirituality.

There have been and are many efforts in this direction. These, too, need guidance and oversight by responsible trained clergy and/or lay leaders with an understanding of the problems with which they are dealing. Some churches have an organization that visits families regularly, beginning with the arrival of a new baby. They offer gentle, mature guidance to the parents on spiritual aspects of child rearing, giving literature for the parents and small religious gifts for the children on special occasions. Such "family visitors" fill the role formerly occupied by godparents in the days when being a godparent was taken seriously and not as an occasional social and ceremonial duty.

Responsible, wise, and caring godparents—whether institutional or personal—can fill a very real need for the many young parents who have grown up without adequate opportunity to learn good parenting skills. Religious communities would do well to revive and promote the practice of serious godparenting, even if those communities have never historically practiced it.

Parents can find many good books and classes to assist them. Fortunately, the teaching of religious parenting seems to be growing from the practice of simply teaching rote prayers and Bible stories (important as they are) to developing a child's sense of self worth, trust, and responsibility toward self, family, others, and God.

Family religious rituals are no less important than they ever were. Indeed in this highly secularized world they are more necessary than ever. But they must be practiced in a climate of love and respect for all the members of the family or they will be just so much sounding brass and tinkling cymbals.

The Religious School

Virtually every religion practiced in the Western world has some form of school for its children. Some of these never get far beyond teaching prayers and Scripture verses and stories. Even then, there is opportunity to help children grow into loving, trusting, confident persons. The following are some specific teaching practices/methods that can be used.

a. Keep the lesson and verses in context and include the historical and cultural contexts in which they were written. It is easy to teach children verses and stories, and easier for them to get the wrong idea. In this, as well as all the areas following, teachers must learn to recognize their own misconceptions and prejudices. The various sides of the picture must be presented and discussed. For example: Christian children need to know the context of Paul's teachings about women in church and marriage in the light of the culture of his time and the full teachings of Jesus about human dignity and sacrificial service for all. They need to learn how Jesus honored and respected women in contrast to the way former cultures had treated females. Jewish children should learn how the culture and attitudes of the past have been supplanted by better knowledge of human behavior and of God's love. In the same way as Christian children need to learn how Jesus brought new dignity to woman, so Moslem children should see how Mohammad made radical departures from past treatment of women. Baha'i children need to know that telling their parents about people who do bad things is not sinful backbiting.

b. Use a wide range of scriptural, historical, and contemporary role models of both sexes and many races. Some of the role models from Scripture are not adequate or applicable to life today. Use of only scriptural or traditional figures of faith sometimes leads children to believe all the good people were in the past or that all of them were so perfect and without spot that no one can ever measure up to them. Such idealized creatures appear to have little relevance to children and young people who know they are not perfect themselves. Use of postscriptural and contemporary persons of both sexes and many different races allows children to see that everyone can be holy and a spiritual hero. This is especially true where female role models for both boys and girls are concerned. Both sexes need to learn that God operates through women in roles other than the traditional ones of someone's wife and someone's mother—and through elderly, fat, disabled, assertive "uppity" women, too.

c. Use of role-playing techniques, where children act out situations in the other person's shoes. This is an excellent technique for teaching respect for others' feelings and ways of thinking. A teacher might have teens and preteens reverse sex roles and lay out stereotypical situations. Role-playing is also a good method for learning nonviolent ways for managing conflict and frustration.

d. Use class participation wherever possible, feeding the child's sense of accomplishment and treating the sexes equally, avoiding stereotyping. Children can come up with surprising wisdom, as all teachers know. Participation in discussion and presentations enables children to gain confidence, but only if all are given an opportunity. It is of utmost importance that sex-role stereotyping be absolutely vanquished from the classroom discussion time. There are two tendencies that are equally demeaning. One is to call on more girls because they seem to be "smarter" and "politer" than boys. The other is to allow boys to interrupt and preempt the floor from the girls. All sex-biased remarks by students must be stopped and explanations given as to why such remarks are wrong and not in accordance with God's will. Cooperation, appreciation of each other's differences and limitations and abilities should replace competition whenever possible. When team activities are used, care should be exercised to see that both sexes are represented on each team. This avoids pitting girls and boys against each other and furthering the impression that the sexes must be on opposing sides.

Class participation situations are also excellent places for teachers to spot signs of abuse. The child who is too disruptive or too quiet, too out of control or too well behaved, the child who seems depressed, hungry, or who shrinks from normal physical contact may be in trouble at home. What happens at home *is* the church's business when it involves the abuse of the children of God (which is all of us).

e. Deal with questions of sexuality and sexual morals in an open, frank manner that allows children to develop a reverence and respect for their bodies and the bodies of others. It is impossible to get through the preteen years without approaching the subject of sexual morality. Such teaching should begin very early with the teaching that the body is the temple of God's Spirit, and that it is to be reverenced, cared for, and protected from anyone who would injure or defile it. No matter what the stand of the particular faith community on matters such as premarital sex, birth control, abortion, homosexuality, etc., respect for one's own body and the bodies of others should be taught in a religious context. Respect for one's own body means the right to say no to any kind of touching that causes feelings of discomfort. (Discomfort does not necessarily include the firm hand on the rear when everything else has failed to keep the three-year old off the freeway!)

Wise and effective teachers should not be surprised when children or teens begin to confide in them privately about abuse or fears. When an atmosphere of understanding and trust has been created, victims will begin to talk about their problems and fears in private. The teacher should be alert to signals that a child or young adult is wrestling with a decision to trust and talk. The teacher must be prepared to listen, without denying or judging, and with the reassurance that help will be made available. Most important, the teacher must have been educated on what then to do with the information.

f. Teach resolution of conflict by nonviolent means, which includes honestly confronting the conflict and resolving it. Scriptural passages can be used as examples of ways in which it was done by Moses, Jesus, and the prophets in their days and how we believe God wishes it to be done now: When it is appropriate to fight like Mohammad and Moses and when the way of peace is required.

Two of the important skills for the teacher to know are mediation and dealing with anger. Children can learn to recognize and deal with perceived threats to their security and dignity that bring forth angry responses. Moreover, many of these methods just use simple fairness and common sense added to some basics of psychology. One does not have to have a counseling degree to learn and use them.

The success of a formal religious education program, however, depends on the teachers and the quality of their training. To quote Iris Cully:[9]

> Too many church school sessions, whether held on Sunday, weekday, or during vacation time, are staffed by volunteers who decry their own limitations yet do not take the steps necessary to become informed teachers. They derive satisfaction from having done a favor for the pastor who was desperate for help and seem not to realize that both their own egos and those of the children would be better sustained by some good hard work. Children want to be motivated . . . want to use new-found skills. . . . But methods alone can be clever and empty.

The Religious Community

The church or religious community has not, on the whole, responded adequately to problems of sexual and domestic violence within it. The feeling among clergy has been that there were no problems. This feeling was the logical result of not having heard about the problems. After all, religious people are supposed to be good people who don't behave in that way. When the religious community has had opportunities to respond constructively to such situations, it has frequently been hesitant, silent, and sometimes destructive in its response, largely due to its limited view of women and marriage. "Go home and pray." "Be a better wife and mother." "Offer it up." Faced with such nonadvice, women quit talking. The silence has been deafening.

It is true that religious leaders and counselors who are unaware of the dynamics of family violence and untrained in dealing with it can—and do make bad situations worse, but the religious community has a responsibility to respond.

First and foremost, religious beliefs and experience are central to people's lives. Deeply or even moderately religious persons will weigh their life experiences in the balance of their religious faith. Second, abuse is happening in the lives of religious people, sometimes caused or contributed to by the kinds of thinking detailed in Part I. A third reason is that if the shepherds do not guide their flocks the wolves will triumph. If God is, then God's representatives must make that presence felt. To continue to ignore or condone the destruction of God's children is blasphemy itself. If there is a devil, how could he be better served than by such failure on the part of the representatives of his Enemy? Fourth, sincerely religious people feel hesitant about going to secular social agencies for help because these agencies often have little or no understanding of, or patience with, religious concerns. Often, too, the victim fears that word may get back to the pastor and the congregation, causing her to be rejected or ostracized.

Someone in the religious community must take the lead in awakening it to the problems before it can work on solutions. That someone may be a member of the clergy (or the persons with pastoral functions in faiths that have no clergy). It may be a member of the elders or the parish council, or the women's organization, or just some concerned members of the community. Whoever takes the lead, the pastor or pastoral body then has the responsibility to educate the community.

Clergy, lay leaders, and counselors may enroll in a workshop or short course, such as those offered by the Center for Prevention of Sexual and Domestic Violence (see Part IV). They may arrange to be trained by a secular agency, university-associated family guidance practitioner, or the like. If no other help is available they may at least read some of the new books on the subject, such as *Sexual Violence, the Unmentionable Sin* (see the references).

Having educated themselves, they can begin to teach the community through inviting guest speakers, sermons, workshops, hiring/appointing trained counselors, special study groups, and initiating programs through existing organizations concerned with marriage and the family. Other actions the religious community can take are becoming familiar with the laws pertaining to domestic and sexual violence, providing printed information for members of the community on where and how to get help, contributing financial or other support to shelters for battered women and rape crisis centers, supporting proposed changes in laws where necessary, and developing support programs within the framework of the community for victims and offenders undergoing treatment.

We must have great sympathy for the pastor who must own up to his/her former inadequacies in presenting Scripture or church teaching. It takes great humility for any of us to admit that we have been wrong or that we may have inadvertently, but with the best of intentions, led others astray. The pastor or pastoral body is the servant of the servants of God, and if that can be kept in mind and heart all of the community will grow and prosper emotionally and spiritually.

Society

The religious community's duty to educate does not end at the doorway of the house of worship. Because God's people are to be the leaven in the larger society, they have a responsibility to God and their fellow men and women. By its visible concern, the religious community can help overcome the conspiracy of silence that has surrounded family violence in the past. The community must clearly assert to the community at large that abuse of persons, especially in the family, is sin. The church must speak out boldly and say that this is not merely a private affair or a religious concern but a problem which affects all of society. To do less is to fail to be about our Father's business.

We must begin also to understand that in our competitive, dehumanizing society we have come to think of and treat people as if they were things: units of labor, units of pleasure, units of consumption. Our society has forced the sexes into an unnatural division of labor. As women seek equality in the business world they are told to suppress-for-success their compassion and feeling and to oppress-for-success, just like men.

Helen Block Lewis, in *Psychic War in Men and Women,*[10]

makes a strong point that women often treat things as people while men tend to treat people as things, with the result that neither men nor women are capable of viewing the world of people *and* things as it is. It would be tragic if the feminist movement simply resulted in reversing the stereotypes. Only the interjection of basic religious values into society can create the climate where true respect, equality, and justice—not to mention true love—can govern the affairs of peoples. What is needed is not the narrowly defined temporal values of particular sects but those eternal spiritual values held by all: the sacredness of all human beings as creations of a loving and just God.

If the people of God do not take on the responsibility of educating humanity, who will?

IV. The National Center for the Prevention of Sexual and Domestic Violence

There are grassroots religious education movements concerned with the questions of domestic and sexual abuse springing up across the country. It would not be possible to list them all here. The first and only major organization specifically designed to train clergy and religious leaders and counselors to deal with these problems within the framework of their own faiths, is the Center for the Prevention of Sexual and Domestic Violence, located in Seattle, Washington. It was founded in 1977 by the Rev. Marie Fortune, a United Church of Christ minister, with assistance from several denominations. The Center also concentrates on educating the secular community, both social work and law enforcement agencies, on the importance of the role played by religious concerns in the lives of victims and abusers.

The Center is now run by Marie Fortune and a small paid professional staff, governed by a fifteen-member board of directors. The board at this writing is composed of women and men representing the Christian, Jewish, and Baha'i faiths. Racial and ethnic minorities, as well as the lesbian and gay communities, are represented. There are plans to expand the board to include more faiths and more minorities. Although the workshop and other training programs now available are aimed at the Christian community, preparation of material for the Baha'i community has begun, and groundwork is being laid for developing Jewish programs.

Although the Center carries on several training programs on a national scale, the heart of the work is the workshop program. Several types of workshops, varied in length, depth, and subject matter, are available at moderate cost to groups desiring them. Courses which train other groups to offer the basic workshops are available on a regional basis. In addition, the Center also publishes a manual: *Family Violence, a Workshop Manual for Clergy and Other Service Providers,* which gives specific instructions for those who wish to give the workshops in their own area. The Center has begun programs for seminaries to educate future clergy-members and thus begin the cycle of religious education for prevention and treatment of domestic and sexual abuse.

Clergy and others wishing to know more about the work of the Center should contact them at the address and phone number shown in the list of references at the end of the chapter.

V. Conclusion

In the beginning the question was asked: "What went wrong?" Now that we know, we have no excuse for failing to make it right. It is not enough to wait for the pastor or the rabbi or the mullah or the priest or the meeting or the elders or the assembly to make it right. It is the duty of all the people of God.

> "Thus says the Lord: 'We have heard a cry of panic, of terror, and no peace!' " *O.T.*, Jeremiah 30:5
> "And He said, 'I am Jesus, whom you are persecuting.' " *N.T.* Acts 9:5
> "We have sent down to you revelations showing you the right path." *The Quran*, Surih 24:34
> "And also in yourselves, will ye not, then behold the signs of God?" *Baha'i World Faith*, p. 117

NOTES

1. Center for the Prevention of Sexual and Domestic Violence, Background material for workshops.
2. Marie M. Fortune, *Sexual Violence, the Unmentionable Sin* (New York: Pilgrim Press, 1983), pp. 44-46.
3. Sally Priesand, *Judaism and the New Woman* (New York: Behrman House, 1975), pp. 3-5, 27.
4. Sarah M. Perkins letter, *The Woman's Bible*, ed. Elizabeth Cady Stanton (Seattle Coalition Task Force on Women and Religion, 1974), p. 212.
5. Josephine K. Henry letter, ibid., p. 194.
6. Fortune, *Sexual Violence*, p. 61.
7. Laura Clifford Barney, *Some Answered Questions* (Baha'i Publishing Trust, 1981 ed.), p. 270.
8. Fortune, *Sexual Violence* p. 229.
9. Iris V. Cully, *Christian Child Development* (New York: Harper & Row, 1979), p. 15.
10. Helen Block Lewis, *Psychic War in Men and Women* (New York: University Press, 1976), p. 93.

REFERENCES

Baha'i Publishing Trust, *Baha'i World Faith*, Wilmette, Ill., 1956 ed.

Barney, Laura Clifford, comp. *Some Answered Questions.* Wilmette, Ill.: Baha'i Publishing Trust, 1981 ed.

Center for the Prevention of Sexual and Domestic Violence, workshop background material. Seattle, Wash., 1979-80.

——. *Family Violence, a Workshop Manual for Clergy and Other Service Providers,* 1980.

Cully, Iris V. *Christian Child Development,* San Francisco: Harper & Row, 1979.

Fortune, Marie M. *Sexual Violence, the Unmentionable Sin.* New York: The Pilgrim Press, 1983.

The Holy Bible, Revised Standard Version. New York: Thomas Nelson & Sons, 1953.

Kemelman, Harry. *Conversations with Rabbi Small.* New York: Fawcett Crest Books, 1982.

The Koran, Dawood Translation. New York: Penguin Books, 1974 ed.

Kushner, Harold S. *When Bad Things Happen to Good People.* New York: Avon, 1983.

Lewis, Helen Block. *Psychic War in Men and Women.* New York University Press, 1976.

Lippman, Thomas W. *Understanding Islam.* New York: Mentor Books, 1982.

May, Gerald G. *Care of Mind, Care of Spirit: Psychiatric Dimensions of Spiritual Direction.* San Francisco: Harper & Row, 1982.

McCuen, Gary E., and Bender, David L., eds. *Opposing Viewpoints Series: The Sexual Revolution.* Minneapolis: Greenhaven Press, 1972.

Mollenkott, Virginia Ramey. *Women, Men and the Bible.* Nashville: Abingdon, 1977.

Price, Eugenia. *God Speaks to Women Today.* Grand Rapids, Mich.: Zondervan, 1964.

Priesand, Sally. *Judaism and the New Woman.* New York: Behrman House, 1975.

Stanton, Elizabeth Cady and the Revising Committee. *The*

Woman's Bible. Seattle: Coalition Task Force on Women and Religion, 1974 (republication).

Waddy, Charis. *The Muslim Mind.* London: Longman, 1976.

The Center for the Prevention of Sexual and Domestic Violence is located at 1914 North 34th Street, Suite #205, Seattle, Wash. 98103. The telephone number is (206) 634-1903.

Chapter 6

Black Women as Professional Religious Educators

ETHEL R. JOHNSON

At a recent meeting of almost a thousand religious educators, I was dismayed to find fewer than twenty black women, only two of whom were employed as full-time professionals in a black local church. This affirmed the conclusion of informal research I had done on black women in religious education: A few are employed full-time in white churches and others are serving full-time on judicatory or agency staffs. Most women in black churches are volunteers and/or part-time. Most religious educators in black churches are not seen as professionals.

Historical Context

This is indicative of the black woman's role in the United States. It is necessary to acknowledge that the black woman has always had two strikes against her—she is black and she is a woman.

> In general the lot of black women under slavery was in every respect more arduous, difficult, and restricted than that of men. Their work and duties were the same as that of men,

115

while childbearing and rearing fell upon them as an added burden. Punishment was meted out to them regardless of motherhood, pregnancy, or physical infirmity. Their affection for their children was used as a deliberate means of tying them to their masters, for children could always be held as hostages in case of the mother's attempted escape. The chances of escape for female slaves were fewer than those for males. Additionally, the sexual exploitation and abuse of black women by white men was a routine practice.[1]

When slave women did not submit to their masters they often would be stripped and beaten in public. Imagine the humiliation! Some mothers preferred to kill their girl babies rather than have them subjected to such indecencies.

Although female slaves' work and duties were the same as that of men, men were the overseers—the bosses. This is the kind of world in which black women are still living today. Our work is often more arduous, difficult, and restricted than that of men and white women. Until the late 1960s there were few black women in managerial positions over men and white women and fewer with higher pay. Unfortunately, this is still so in the church—especially with black women religious educators. Today as I've talked with black women religious educators who are employed full-time by black churches, I find that most of them who are not Black Baptist have their employment because of outside grants. Is the black church so poor that it cannot afford religious educators? This is true for some, but there are others who have the money but do not have religious education as a priority.

A black woman who will graduate in June with a masters degree in religious education is desperately looking for employment in a black local church. She has offers in white churches and on judicatory and agency staffs, but she feels called to share her gifts and graces with black people.

Some reasons for this dilemma are: (1) We live in a sexist society—women's work is not considered as important as men's, and normally religious education in a local church is seen as women's work. (2) Many black pastors do not place a premium on religious education. Worship and preaching are the hub of church life. (3) Religious education is seen as too narrow a focus so another cleric is hired when an additional staff person is needed. This person may be given the responsibility for religious education—an area in which s/he may not be (usually is not) trained. (4) There are many women volunteers in religious education in the church so they continue to work.

With this background, why would any self-respecting black woman want to become a religious educator? Let me share my story.

A Black Religious Educator

Through the years the church has been the mainstay of my life. In spite of the degradation I experienced in the secular world and in some religious circles, I knew I was a person of worth in the eyes of God, my family, and most members of the congregation.

I was surrounded with role models of strong black women volunteer religious educators. Their teaching techniques were not the most appropriate for my inquisitive mind, but I felt their love for me. I *happily* participated in the monthly Sunday School get-togethers, Vacation Bible School, picnics, and youth institutes. I *endured* Sunday School, worship, and Christmas pageants.

But there was more to church life than that. It was in church that I heard about the injustices experienced by black people and the importance of our joining together in working for justice. Here I was taught not to hate but not to endure passively either. It was in this context that I joined the adults of the congregation in attempting to eliminate overt racism.

Social work was going to be my vocation so that I could equip others to fight for self-determination. In the midst of the second year of my social work studies I suddenly realized I was in the wrong graduate school! I needed to be a director of religious education! There was no "burning bush," no "sudden blindness," no "time in the belly of a whale"—just a realization of what I was to do with my life and where to go for the necessary training.

Why religious education? Grant Shockley defines Christian (religious) education in the black church as: "that process which teaches concepts, attitudes, and skills which facilitate meaningful learning in relation to the black experience and the church's implicit task of humanization and liberation."[2] His definition is contemporary, but the intent is a part of what motivated me over thirty years ago. If religious teachings do not facilitate learnings in relation to black people's experiences as black people—the teachings are "head trips" only. If the black local church is not engaged in tasks of humanization and liberation, it is not training for discipleship. I knew I needed to be on the cutting edge of the humanization, liberation struggle and that a theological background was essential preparation.

As a black woman in a predominantly white seminary, I had a difficult time securing a field placement in a black church since I refused to be placed in a white church. Finally, I was told that if I could find a church the school would certify it. I did. The humanization struggle had begun! (Today, as director of field education at a predominantly white seminary, I find myself struggling to find placements for black women students in black churches. Will the struggle never end?)

Finding employment in a black church as a black woman with a masters degree in religious education is challenging.

When I graduated from seminary my home church employed me. This was made possible with a grant from the predominantly white judicatory of which the church was a part.

After serving in a local church I joined our judicatory staff. There was one other staff person—a white clergyman. I was treated as an equal and my ministry was rewarding. After two years, another younger, less-experienced white clergyman was added to the staff. In working out a salary package for him it was discovered that my salary would have to be greatly increased and hospitalization and pension benefits added to make it *equal* to his. It was done. No one had thought about the injustice—not even me, because I was enjoying my job.

As a member of the faculty of a theological school, I continue to work at the religious educator's task to humanize and liberate.

Peculiar Difficulties

The greatest difficulty I find in working beyond black local churches is the expectations of white colleagues that I represent and speak for all blacks—not always for all women—but for all blacks. Too frequently, my colleagues feel they are absolved from having to include black experiences and people in their responsibilities because I'm there; I "set the record straight."

It is lonely being the "only one": the only director of religious education on a black or white church staff; the only black on an all-white staff; the only woman on an all-male staff. I have been in all three situations. Therefore, it has been and continues to be imperative for me to build a support system for survival. Mine usually has been with people outside my place of employment. For six years it was a group of religious educators (mostly black) who covenanted to meet for breakfast and study on a monthly basis. Presently it is with a group of nineteen other religious educators from across the country who meet twice a year for study and fellowship and with four white couples (I am single) who meet twice a month for study and fellowship.

Most of the phone calls I receive from black women religious education graduates are out of their loneliness and lack of humanization—especially if the woman is single. We are a couple-oriented society, and single people have to fight for the right to exist as equals. The struggle goes on.

Sometimes it is difficult to determine whether one's loneliness and frustration is due to racism or sexism or both. Not being heard as a part of a staff is an example of the situation. A black woman makes a suggestion and the discussion continues as if she hasn't spoken. A man can make a similar suggestion later on, and it is received as exciting new data.

Being expected to do a "woman's work" is another example. Taking minutes, getting coffee, making the phone calls, sending the thank-you notes, getting appreciation gifts—all with a smile after receiving a pat on the head or derriere—is degrading. Being referred to as a "girl" is insulting. I have learned to cope better as I have become more liberated from within. I say "no" when I feel the task is given to me because I am a woman and I don't want to do it. I say "yes" to the things I enjoy doing whether I consider it women's work or not.

Peculiar Opportunities

You may want to ask then, "Why would any self-respecting black woman continue to work as a religious educator?"

I ask myself that question frequently to remind myself of what I am about. And I must admit that there have been some days when I could not bring myself to sing, "We Shall Overcome." Sometimes, the task of humanization and liberation seemed so overwhelming that I have found it hard to believe we shall overcome.

Yet, in spite of the frustrations, there is an excitement and challenge to being a religious educator in the black church that cannot be equaled. The unique opportunity it provides has been succinctly captured by Olivia Stokes.

> The black church has been the most powerful force of the black people's struggle for justice, equality, liberation, and freedom. . . . The power of the black church is in "people power" and "presence" and provides the richest sources of ethically motivated leadership, lay and clergy, in the black community.[3]

She goes on to quote Dr. Benjamin E. Mays:

> The black church is always pointing black people to a better day, both in the present and in the future.[4]

The field of religious education has always been a source of what is done best in black churches. Unlike the educational programs in most other churches, it has never confined itself to instruction in doctrine. Its concerns have been much broader, but always grounded in a solid theological base. A few personal memories will illustrate the point.

I remember with delight abandoning the two-week vacation Bible school that had traditionally been a summer event. We had concentrated the previous year on enabling people to articulate their needs. They did. They decided that what they needed was not the typical VBS but rather a two-month, five-days-a-week, seven-hours-a-day program that would prepare the older youth for leadership. They got it.

Senior high-school youth went through a week-long training period to prepare them to be leaders for the younger people when they arrived. These youth continued to be treated as leaders through the summer, not as helpers. Moreover, they modeled this leadership to their younger brothers and sisters. That seemed to be all the motivation they needed to *relish* their responsibility. There was no problem with absenteeism or punctuality during that grueling program.

The biblically based program on stewardship that was offered that summer typifies the broad-based character of religious education in the black church. A group of six-year-olds went into the local store of a supermarket chain to purchase two pounds of chopmeat. They were told to observe the cleanliness of the store, the friendliness and courtesy of the employees, as well as the price of their purchase. Then they were taken across town to a store of the same chain, to make the same purchase and the same observations. When they returned, they cooked both packages of meat and compared their observations. They learned that in their part of the town, the meat cost more, had more fat in it, and, as they said, "smelled funny." They were beginning their education in the "struggle for justice, equality, liberation, and freedom." And it was religious education.

Another memory that convinces me of the inestimable value of religious education, and also illustrates its unique character in the black church is that of women staying up all night to finish making uniforms for a drum and bugle corps. A talented local layman who had himself been a member of a high-school corps, offered to teach and direct any interested young people unable to pay for lessons, much less for instruments. Through a myriad of projects, money was raised to buy instruments. All that was needed for their debut were the uniforms. Women who could not sew learned how to that night from those who could. The corps members learned the discipline and cooperation to become a successful unit. "People power" and "presence" were being galvanized. And it was religious education.

In the black church, religious education involves one in the processes that teach attitudes, concepts, and skills which facilitate meaningful learning in relation to the black experience and the church's implicit task of humanization and liberation. Perhaps the most fundamental attitude, concept, and skill that is taught is the equality of all people. In one church that education was lived out by everyone—clergy and lay—acting as if they were equal.

It is hard to feel equal when there are indicators all around that you are not. Even the good intentions of white people wanting to do things for black people perpetuates the implication that all black people are poor and needy. After engaging in biblical and theological study on the nature of the church, this local church developed a purpose statement that proclaimed the equality of all as created by God and demonstrated by Jesus. At some point it became obvious to everyone that they should be acting as if they were equal to each other, and so the barriers of clergy and lay collapsed.

They all shared the dreaming and planning as well as the implementation. They also modeled this equality to a white church that had seen itself as "helping" their black sisters and brothers by assisting with salaries, donating old curricula, etc. The two churches began to meet for *joint* dreaming and planning and implementation. Activities began to be done "with" each of the churches, not "for" either of them.

Conclusion

If ever religious educators needed to be professionally prepared and professionally employed and professionally paid, that need exists in the black church. Until now the burden has fallen on the shoulders of volunteers, almost all of whom are women. As a result, they have their whole other "women's" life to which they must attend in addition to their church work. They have families to raise, homes to keep, and, too frequently, salaries to earn.

The "women's work" of religious education must be seen for what it is: fundamental to the mission of the church. The commission to the apostles and disciples was first of all to "teach . . ." (Mt. 28:20). This need is not peculiar to black churches, of course.

But black pastors must make religious education a priority in their budgets as well as encourage promising members of their congregations to prepare themselves professionally. It is particularly urgent in today's world where racism and injustice are as rampant as ever, but more subtle, perhaps, in many of their manifestations.

Finally, black women religious educators must band together for the mutual support they need in a world where to be black and female is still a double burden, and where, in the black church, their work is still the main source of the humanization and liberation process. Perhaps, even more urgently, we must call and prepare our sisters to enter the fray.

NOTES

1. Gerda Lenner, *Black Women in White America* (New York: Random House, 1972), p. 15.
2. Grant Shockley, *Christian Education and the Black Church* (Nashville: Discipleship Resources, 1985), p. 2.

3. Olivia Pearl Stokes, "Black Theology: A Challenge to Religious Education," in *Religious Education and Theology,* ed. Norma H. Thompson (Birmingham, Ala.: Religious Education Press, 1982), pp. 84, 85.
4. Benjamin E. Mays, *The Negro's God as Reflected in His Literature* (Boston: Chapman and Grimes, 1938), cited in *Religious Education and Theology,* p. 85.

Chapter 7

Structure and Process

FERN M. GILTNER

Women's Place in Society

I mentioned in the preface of this book that my purpose in writing about women in theological school structure is to focus on the structure of academic institutions as an example of the structure of most social institutions in the United States.

I choose to write about institutional structure because I believe that women have been "structured" out of society except in supportive roles and in the one institution of the home.

According to Laurel Richardson Walum, sociologist and author of *The Dynamics of Sex and Gender: A Sociological Perspective,* all modern industrial societies have social stratification systems. She also points out that socially structured inequity is a fundamental feature of social life.[1]

Women are realizing that, at least since the Industrial Revolution in our country, society has been structured into two very different systems. One system has been designated as women's world and responsibility and the other system has been designated as men's world and responsibility.

These two worlds are actually two different cultures interdependent but separate. The world of women is the private world of home and men's world is the public world of work, vocation, and economics. This dualistic structuring has enabled an unfair division of labor and power.

And if industrialization of our country is responsible for the development of labor as we know it, it is the sexual stratification that has maintained the system.

The public world of work has been given the dominant role and has the responsibility to maintain the private world of home as well as the public world since the power resides in the public world. That is, some persons in the economic world have the power to make the decisions that affect the lives of everyone in the country because they have control of the needed goods and services and the distribution of them. Since it is men who are to live and work in the public world and it is women who are to live in the private world, it is not difficult to document sexual stratification and the ensuing problem of inequity.

Since socially structured inequity is so basic a part of our life, we are prone to accept it as inevitable. Also, the structure is maintained as long as persons accept their prescribed place in the order.

As a religious educator, I would like to think that we are no longer prescribing gender roles (or any other group role). However, experience confirms that persons' roles and places go with them as they become part of the world of work. We are still enculturating persons through our homes, our language, our schools, mass media, and religious institutions to know what is normal and what is expected of them as members of their sex.

The dualistic social structure of two worlds, one for men and one for women and children has resulted in two economic systems. Walum points out that "the system is structured such that the extradomestic advantage gained by men can be used to purchase the domestic services of women."[2] Women's work in the world of home has not been compensated by any monetary reward and therefore has no "real" value. When a woman enters the public world of work and receives a salary her work is still of no real value for she is seen as out of place and thought to be temporary or supportive. As long as society believes the myth that places women in a separate world she will be treated as "other" and society can fool itself.

This patriarchal system and mind-set is particularly vicious since a large percentage of women do not live with men; they support themselves and yet they are subject to the economic system that does not consider women's work to be as valuable as men's and thus pays less for their labor. The feminization of poverty in our society is one of the most crucial issues for our society and for religious education to face.

But today women consider work as a career or a way of living. They are not "filling in" or "helping out" in any way. They enter the world of work with a goal and a purpose that is no less than men's purposes have always been.

It does not take long to realize that those "in charge" do not willingly share power, position, or money and that their structures are not like women's structures. The system has been organized for men and their prescribed role and characteristics, and women are placed at a distinct disadvantage. The laddered structure of authority and power is able to control one's life and spirit. Women's enculturation, their experience and development, their ways of learning and working have been left out of this system. Women begin to realize that their integrity and authenticity is at stake. They do not want to give up their way of relating which has been their way of structure. Women believe that their world, too, has been the "real" world and it also is valuable.

If the hierarchical and patriarchal structure of the work world is built on the dicotomy of the value of male and female, it creates a dualistic and alienating worldview patterned on the basic inequity of power and authority. Our culture will have to believe that women and men are both responsible for earning money and making decisions in the world of economics and politics and also that men and women are both responsible for rearing the children and keeping the home if both sexes are to have an equal opportunity to be whole persons with free choices. Would this make it possible to reconstruct a more inclusive worldview of creation and humanity so that neither men nor women would be called on to choose between home and family relationships and being part of the social and economic system? If so, both men and women would have a voice in making the decisions that involve human welfare. The divisions in our cultural structure must somehow be healed and integrated.

We are in the process of great change in our world, and it is causing strain on the structure of society. Religious educators are constantly observing and reevaluating reality and human experience. Today books are written on the importance of human contact in the day of computerization. Some corporations are experimenting with more egalitarian systems of organization. We are called on to work together as we find the source of strength and empowerment within ourselves and beyond our human limitations. Our educational structure and religious images need to be inclusive and mutually integrative to enable all persons to receive clear vision and purpose and wholeness of identity. Structure built on inequity bruises and disintegrates as it denies the fullness of divine love. This calling is the nature of religious education.

I hope to show the importance of systemic change in all institutions by discussing women's entry into theological schools. Academic schools are part of the public world of work as well as part of the realm of scholasticism.

What happens to women as they enter a theological school system has parallels in any patriarchal institution and any school of higher education for they have been institutions for men only. As women enter any field of work that has been men's domain, there is an imbalance and a necessity for change and development and mutual accommodation.

Women in Theological Schools

The year was probably 1975.

The scene was a theological school cafeteria.

A professor was talking with me because I worked with women students. As a friend who cared for the students, he asked me to "put the women's concerns and issues into systematic theological language so that I can respond to them theologically."

What a strange request. Women had been meeting together for a couple of years sharing experiences, books, ideas, and putting words on their feelings. In this struggle and collaboration they were gaining new insights and learning from each other as they affirmed the ways, the strengths, and the beliefs of women. They agreed on words and ways of expressing their thoughts and care. They needed each other for support in this somewhat alien place and they were discovering their voices and the empowerment of sisterhood. They encouraged each other and developed a strong belief in the value of and the determination to own the validity of their way of working and knowing, and yes, of theologizing.

Here were women in a theological school determined to take their rightful place in ministry, working for all the necessary credentials of the system, doing excellent work academically and, who, in many cases, were bringing to the seminary years of theological reflection and the practice of ministry. This question from the professor seemed to be an anomaly. We were asked to fit our issues, our concerns, into authentic, systematic, and acceptable theology. It was as though our knowledge of God, our faith statements, were other than theology, as though they were not valid. Surely theology is not bound by any one system.

Of course, women conformed to the system, and it was not difficult to theologize systemically and in the traditional way. They proved their ability to do the academic work and many received excellent grades. In fact with the advent of women in theological schools, the grade-point average was raised much to everyone's amazement and pleasure. To be accepted in a foreign culture one must do more and prove more ability in order to demonstrate equality and worth. When I was in college from 1945 to 1949, I had friends who were Japanese-American. They never wasted a minute. Their reason for needing to prove their excellence was due to their racial heritage in the aftermath of World War II. Women still have to prove that they are intelligent and that they have validity as a trustworthy candidate for the world of work versus the world of home and domesticity.

But women became conscious of a difference in their development and socialization from that of the men students. They seemed to perceive differently and even to speak and to write in a different language. Choosing to own the difference and see it as a strength and not as a weakness, women struggled for a clearer vision for imaging God's power in their lives. They continued to meet for support and struggled together and their shared faith became stronger; they began to name their faith experience and images and symbols and own their language of speaking of divinity and spirituality and connection.

Communication and Connection

Women are finding that they are not willing to give up the connections between their lives and the lives of other women nor their ways of communication. That cultural connection has made them who they are. Sharing of time and empowerment and close relationships make women affirm their distinctiveness as women. Women have learned their lesson from the culture of the private world of home and find that the values learned from their experience work creatively and they believe them to be needed in the culture of the public world of work.

Jean Baker Miller, a noted psychologist, helps women understand that affiliation is a basic strength and that development and growth depend on it.[3] She also affirms women's qualities of cooperation, creativity, dealing emotionally, willingness to live with change, caring for others even during conflict, as valuable psychological qualities. She states that Western society may have reached "a point from which we must return to a basic of faith in affiliation—and not only faith but recognition that it is a requirement for the existence of human beings."[4] She sees women's characteristics and structuring to be helpful in offering the "motivation and direction for moving on."[5]

It takes time to believe that one's commitment to include everyone, insistence on the importance of keeping relationships sacred, tendencies to be indirect and tentative, and making generalizations are acceptable traits and are valuable and that it is all right to keep them. They can seem to be weaknesses in the work world when they are compared to traits such as seeming to be certain, exact, aggressive, and competitive. However, we are affirming our style of communication as a strength since it reflects our style of affiliating and relating.

Women's perspective is not synonomous with the traditional point of view because they did not have a place in shaping the traditional structure. Women have developed some new names, images, and procedures in the religious community that need to be integrated with traditional views. Our more inclusive imaging and naming speaks to the same faith. Women's ways of expressing their ideas include subjectivity and are not the way of academic discourse when it demands detached objectivity and reason without personal experience. As women have found that their unique way of communicating grows out of a unique way of connecting, they hope for change toward some relaxing of the structure and organization of academia so that their way of expressing themselves will be seen as legitimate.

In meetings, our communicating is still relational. In fact, even in business our relationships remain the focus. Rigidity and formal procedures are not the only way to conduct business or to make decisions or to teach and learn. How efficient is making decisions by use of majority vote when many are not encouraged to voice an opinion nor heard nor understood if they try to participate? Women often think they are not understood in meetings. Women do express themselves from a different thought pattern sometimes, but it is also possible that they are not understood because they are not expected to make an important contribution and especially not unless they are of acceptable status with proven excellence and expertise, and unless their contribution fits the structured criteria. Any structure needs to make it possible to communicate with persons of other classes, cultures, races, or religions. We are realizing that not all persons learn, develop, or perceive in one particular pattern, but all deserve a fair, inclusive hearing whatever one's background, goals, lifestyle, gifts, and graces, and sometimes we all unwittingly deny others that basic right.

Need for Structural Change

In 1973, the climate for women in theological schools was pleasant enough and tolerant. But it was a man's world and as women enrolled in classes, women reported the feeling of patronization. They seemed to be "other" and in a less than open, changing system. Thus the words "marginal" or "peripheral" began to be heard. It did "raise consciousness" to be addressed as "fellas" and "men" in classes and worship. It has been said that it also made feminists of many women. The uniqueness of having women in classes and in community has changed the ethos of the schools, but change in structure, ideology, or values is slow. The need for change became clearer when what surely can be viewed as the "critical mass" materialized and one of three students in class was a woman. I understand "critical mass" to define the time when there are enough persons present from a particular group, class, sex, race to be considered as normal phenomena rather than as "token" persons who only maintain stereotypes. Until 1975-76, women were exceptions and those who voiced discontent were trivialized. There were few models of women's leadership in ministry.

Between 1972 and today the number of women entering

many theological school degree programs soared from 5 percent to somewhere between 33 and 50 percent and more in some schools. That all of these women have been placed in ministry in religious institutions after graduation should not be concluded, however, for that logical conclusion is more honestly a confusion than a reality.

The larger the percentage of women, the more resistance is felt when structure is challenged. The institutions welcome women students and mean to treat them equally and take them seriously, but this requires that women's new perspectives must be integrated into the life of the community and classroom and not diagnosed to fit into the traditional pattern.

Women's need for more voice in academic institutions stems partly from the fact that they were not thought to be important enough or intelligent enough to be schooled in this country until the 1800s. Female education was not built into the structure of the social system. Even today two-thirds of illiterate people in the world are female.[6] Education and training in developing countries are still most often offered to men. Women are certainly not a part of the development of academic institutions.

Sociologist and author of *The Female World*, Jessie Bernard, documents that there was a small trickle of women in college in the United States in 1870. By 1978 one-half of college students were women.[7] Women's studies offer the main channel for what Bernard calls the "remarkable corpus of feminist scholarship" which is discovering, exploring, interpreting, and analyzing the female world itself.[8]

But equal access to school does not automatically bring equal education or equal treatment or encouragement. From boys and girls in elementary school to men and women in college and graduate school the educational experience for the sexes differs even in the same classrooms and

with the same instructors. It is believed that different expectations for females and for males play a major role in
limiting female students' development and choices. Barbara Wheeler, president of Auburn Theological Seminary
wrote in an article, "Accountability to Women in Theological Seminaries":

> The feminist perspective asserts that knowledge is condition-
> ed, shaped, and limited by the social location and cultural
> conditioning of those who create knowledge and that it is far
> more difficult to transcend the limits placed by social and
> cultural conditioning than we Western rationalists have long
> thought.[9]

Wheeler maintains that while there are other critical perspectives in theology today, feminists are present "in force"
in seminaries and by "recognizing the vitally important
intellectual and theological challenge of women in theology" the seminaries can best be accountable to women.[10]

Change and Resistance to Change

By 1984, women are more at home in theological
schools. Generic spoken language is in process of change.
Less often is "mankind" or "brotherhood" used. Ministers
are not so often referred to as "he." While there has been
progress, feminists are more and more conscious of how
pervasive is the effect of the sexist English language on
women. Jessie Bernard speaks of the language as hostile to
women and delineates how language not only has been
sexually denigrating and subordinating but it has handi-
capped women by its inadequacy for expressing our experience.[11] It affects their self-image, and it has structured
and limited their world.[12] Religious language must make
room for women's new words, thought patterns, and inclu-

sive images. This is doubly difficult because the English language is not an inclusive language.

Inclusive reading of Scripture and God language have not received as positive a hearing. Feelings still are aroused when feminists question the exclusivity of the male image of God and the use of sexist language in worship.

Inclusion of Women's Studies and Contributions in Curriculum

Course bibliographies usually include texts and research by women scholars. It is hoped that this research will be integrated into all course work and studied by all students. To recognize and analyze the now obvious gap of women's story and contribution in religious tradition necessitates some restructuring of foundational courses.

Elizabeth Langland and Walter Gove, the editors of a volume titled *A Feminist Perspective in the Academy,* say that women's studies have brought a feminist perspective into the academy. But to the questions: Has it transformed curriculum? Has it reshaped materials? Has it altered knowledge? they answer:

> We found that feminist analyses have begun to alter scholarship, but women's studies has yet to have a substantial influence on the traditional curriculum, principally because such analyses challenge fundamental assumptions in each discipline.[13]

Women scholars in all fields of religion have researched, discovered, and documented a considerable library of important contributions and an alternative tradition to fill gaps in the ecclesiastical story so that the inclusion of women and of women's ideas, influence, and worth can be part of the religious heritage and correct the bias of the male-defined theological tradition. Women's experiences and history cannot be left out of the analytical studies. They are part of our heritage and must be added officially. This new scholarship and women's ideas and experiences are a source of content and a part of religious knowledge. Traditional resources and expertise are not being rejected by feminists. The historical-critical model can make room for women's reflection and expression.

Nontraditional methodology may need to become more acceptable, for women learn by expressing their reflections and ideas through creative writing and art, poetry, journals, and storytelling, as well as through scholastic writing. Women seem to need to be involved with the subject matter and to use their own experience as a base for understanding and theologizing.

Her assigned role as a nurturer has caused her to be a generalist and to need to integrate her experience. An interdisciplinary approach is more her style than specialization. She integrates practical skills and affective learning with cognitive learning into a wholistic learning. To separate aspects of learning and reality into domains presents the old dichotomy of what and who is more important.

The structure of academic disciplines and a set criteria for objective scholarship including the nature of research and method is becoming more flexible as the student body becomes more diverse. Some women and men resist a structure with fixed criteria when faced with a diverse community who bring unique contributions to scholarship. Inequities become apparent because of the traditional status of women and because her perspective on teaching and learning has not been part of producing the standard scholastic studies. Including women's studies and critiques will give students a better understanding of humanity and divinity.

A number of theological schools have included specific courses in women's studies in the curriculum. These courses tend to be thought of as peripheral courses and are elected by women. They are often seen as tacked on and not as part of the core curriculum. They do not change the structure of the curriculum of the school. However, they may well be necessary until women's studies are integrated into traditional studies.

The study of sexism is included in specific, elective courses in liberation theology, biblical hermenutics, women in religious history, and similar studies. It is included to some degree in required courses in any discipline, but it will take a more concentrated effort by women in theological schools and all academic schools to effect change in curriculum structure so that women's studies are included as a normal part of the curriculum.

It becomes a political process to be involved in trying to change existing structure and to move education toward wholeness and mutuality. It means that persons in places of power in institutions will have to want to work with women and to be part of a sincere endeavor to evaluate curriculum matters and administrative matters and community life and ourselves for we all need to change and to repent. This calls for sharing power and leadership.

There are more who are women professors and administrators in theological schools now, and they are able to have a voice in decision making and to serve as role models for students. There are women in local church ministry and in a few judicatory offices to serve as role models. But women deserve a central place with men in religious institutions and can no longer accept marginality and limited placement. Women are addressing the need for a fairer proportion of women on faculties and in high-level administrative positions. With some changes and progress, women must not be fooled by believing the system has changed. The systematic nature of sexism must be eliminated and not covered up.

Consciousness Raising and Diversity of Women Students

As women enter theological schools today, they enter different schools than women entered ten years ago. They are not isolated and sexism is less blatant. But many are not aware that others paid a price for them. They may not realize how few women are able to get where they are. They may not see the pain of women in religious faiths that still exclude women from entering the ordained ministry. They will learn that it is still unique to be a woman in ministry and that they will not walk into churches as clergy without confronting obstacles because of gender. Judicatories and local congregations do not yet take clergy who are women as seriously as they do the men. Women are still seen "in relationship to men." Boards and committees will ask more personal questions about leadership style and personal appearance and plans for marriage or willingness to move and for their plans for caring for their children and homes while ministering. Women are not as easily placed as men in required field experience or contextual education or as student pastors or interns while they are students. It will take a long time for ministry to be seen as an appropriate role and profession for women.

In *Women of the Cloth,* the authors Jackson W. Carroll, Barbara Hargrove, and Adair T. Lummis have compiled information from interviews from nine Protestant denominations and present an analysis of clergywomen as compared to clergymen.

They point out that clergywomen report relative success

but some persisting inequities. The most obvious cause of the inequities is the persistence of sexism. They speak of individual sexism as an attitude of nonacceptance of women in ministry and also of institutional sexism. They mention three issues of institutional sexism:

1. Paying clergywomen less than clergymen for similar positions and years of experience.

2. Typecasting of women into particular kinds of clergy positions and keeping them in those kinds of positions so that they do not advance.

3. Continued use of masculine religious language for it shapes consciousness and behavior in the direction of excluding women from ministry.[14]

They also point out the importance of overcoming naivete with realism and wisdom for women entering ordained ministry in order to cope and to effect change. They believe "silent interpenetration" is a slow means of bringing about change. They are referring to just being women in ministry and thinking the church will accept the change and get used to them. They think other "more immediate and effective ways" to speed up the process are necessary. They see "active, vocal women and men advocating for full acceptance of women as ordained ministers to be crucial if the process is not to be interminably slow."[15]

They report the need for judicatory officials to press for acceptance of women in ministry and in all positions of church leadership and on all levels of leadership. Also they believe that "continuing if sometimes irritating advocacy is needed to rid church practices, language, and cultural images of sexism.[16]

Seminary faculty and administration are extremely helpful in recommending and supporting women graduates in church placement. It is particularly important therefore that they see that it is normal and thrilling for women to be in professional ministry.

The boards of trustees of theological schools need to be advocates for women in ministry, and it is important that they elect women members who are aware of the need for structural change in theological schools and who will raise important issues of inclusivity and bring a perspective from women.

However, right now some women in seminaries choose to feel included and part of the structure, and they do not want feminists to point out sexism and racism. Some think of feminists as radical and that their cause is overdone. Though feminists are sometimes resented even by other women, the systemic nature of sexism must continue to be addressed or even feminists will become part of the system that oppresses women.

Administrative Support Staff

When we are speaking of women in theological schools we know that the support staff of the institution has always been primarily women. These positions are vitally important to any institution. They are positions that can be structured and described as dead-end and can be easily filled by anyone with the required skills. Or they can be structured as positions with possibilities for advancement and merit with support for continuing education, growth, and enhancement. Persons who fill this position will feel used and transient if not fairly and equally included and accepted in the community affairs and the school policy. Their salary and benefits, their actual voice and vote in school issues, and their evaluation of their job description, of their working conditions, of their feelings of being pressured, of the expectations placed on them by those with whom they work are of utmost importance.

Women are learning that as we affirm our style of ministry, of teaching/learning, of administration, and our style of working and living together as one of mutuality and cooperation, we have to practice the inclusivity that we defend. That means hearing diverse perspectives of women and binding ourselves together as one people as we work for balance and a renewed understanding of a community of equals. Women need to learn together as we recover and accept our heritage of strength as well as oppression, rejoice in each other's successes, explore our differences, practice listening with honesty and openness, expect conflict and negotiation. If we believe religious faith heals and empowers women, we will affirm our distinctiveness and accept all women.

I have read and agree that when feminism is persistent and insists on inclusion, the reaction from traditionalists is also persistent. Change is hard, and power does not easily share its position. When women want to share their relational and experiential gifts with the world of work and its institutions and find that it causes a resistance from the persons in power and control, it is hard to know how to react. To be trivialized and patronized in religion or any chosen profession is overwhelming, and you begin to realize that asking to be included is divisive.

It is still upsetting in the culture of United States for women to insist on being equal humans with men and not "other" or "helpful" but as normal a human as he. To present as valid and equal women's ways of working with people, of perceiving life as connection to others and cyclical and many layered rather than linear and hierarchic is disruptive. Then to want to change the past norm of methodology, structure, and objectives in teaching and learning in traditional academia is too threatening to acknowledge. The shield of protection and ownership is unmistakably present.

Some Specific Differences in Style of Working

Many women teachers, because of their very relationality, seem to feel ill at ease behind the podium. Chairs in rows for students to sit upon and the teacher standing so that he/she can be heard and seen may be effective for some, but women have always sat in circles or around tables when teaching in religious groupings or other women's study groups and even at home. In religious education as well as in many classrooms in public education, the use of centers of learning, tables for a few students, semicircles and other free and informal settings are the normal and preferred practice. When teaching or leading a group, either peers or children, we have shared with them and listened to their contributions and leveled with a willingness to learn as they learn. There is a set-apart and awkward feeling being up on a platform or behind a lecturn as though performing and taking an authoritative role. We have always looked people in the eye in order to make contact and think with them. In order to build a reciprocal trust and appreciation we need to be on the same level and sit with the students. When working with preschoolers (an important experience for anyone) we automatically kneel down so that we can see each other's eyes. "Who wants to talk to kneecaps" as the saying goes, or never to be the talker and to be distant and segregated from the talker. A circle of persons, no matter how large, or a staggered circle, or a number of circles for sharing and reporting is good teaching practice.

Women do not easily speak with certitude and absolute fact or undeniable revelation. We carry over into the classroom our informal way of communicating and talking. Most women as teachers are functional, authentic listeners and sharers rather than absolute authorities on their specific subject. Again, the desire to include and accept, even encourage, any tentative or indirect or imprecise response is important in teaching/learning theory.

Another difference in style is the importance traditionally placed on titles and degrees and specific placement by divine calling. Some women are finding that form to be stiff and segregating and threatening for students. Our informal style in working in leagues, unions, support groups, reading clubs, study groups, and classes for all types of learning includes addressing all persons there by their given name. The leader, if there is one, introduces herself by her given name. Members have expertise in various areas but each relates as another woman and learns from the other and dispenses information freely. There is no sense of being separate because of being better informed. Efficiency, expertise, and clear outlines are not our main goals, though we have definite purposes and objectives. Titles and robes and vestments are an obvious form that excludes and sets apart. The dualistic view of special placement for those who have power and status seems intentional. The one who wears the robes and carries the title is superior and in a higher class and must be honored and set apart. Father, Reverend, Bishop, Doctor, Mister President, Your Excellency, Your Honor . . . are all forms of distinction and distancing and placing people in social stratification. A judge or a surgeon or the superintendent can lose their humanness if they forget who they are and see their "work" or "vocation" as their identity.

Another use of titles that separates is the insistence to formally address persons in class or in introductions or on mail envelopes with a title such as Mr., Dr., Miss, Mrs., Ms. The formality has been used to show respect *and status* and one's given name was too personal to be used indiscriminately, but it serves again to keep distance, to be less friendly, and it has been a major way to discriminate. Servant classes were called by their first names and never given a title. Doctors and receptionists and psychiatrists, therapists, etc., often call patients or clients that they have never seen before by first names. I approve and prefer that, but I reserve the right to ask their first name also so I can respond in kind. Women have boxes to check on forms so that it can be ascertained if they are married or single. Ms. is fairly well accepted now so that both single and married women can have only one title as men do. Surely a woman need not be known as attached to a husband or a father. She can stand as an authentic person in her own right. We need to continue to make an issue of names and titles. They carry a lot of weight and cause a lot of separation in our culture.

Classes of students and instructors need to be on a first-name acquaintance immediately for maximum learning possibilities. An instructor that I observe starts her new classes by having all class members learn everyone's first name. Each person tells something about her/his name in order to set the name in others' minds. It works wonders to level and include and build relationships.

The egalitarian endeavor as a way to teach and learn with inclusivity and affirmation leads to trust, openness, and mutual respect. Everyone has the opportunity for growth and conversion in an ongoing group experience where all care for each other and take responsibility for her/his own learning and for the class process. Power can be shared and originate in the class as well as in the instructor. There is conflict and exposure but that is acceptable among friends who know each other on a first-name basis. Consensus is not always reached, but each person may be heard. Measurement and evaluation also necessarily are shared.

Women who are ministers or/and students bring unique gifts with them. The reports from many women who have been serving as professional clergy for a few years usually record success and that they are happy in their work, but they often comment on the lack of being imaged as "authority" in the same way as their men colleagues seem to be. They soon decide that this is no problem and that their acceptance comes with function and authenticity.

Women work differently and are finding that they must create their own style and integration and not pattern it on previous models of leadership. They are proving to be particularly sensitive to persons who are oppressed and to persons in the church who need counsel and encouragement. Their administrative style may be less structured and more relaxed and collegial. They are innovative and inclusive in worship and preaching as well. They may take some getting used to, but they model a wholistic life for the congregation.

Conclusion

This chapter has meant to point out that there are real differences in the development and perspective of women and men and that they need to be faced squarely in all institutions including the academy and even theological schools. Women are challenging their culturally ascribed place in the social order and the social system of sexism while insisting on keeping and affirming women's perspectives and relational lifestyle.

NOTES

1. Laurel Richardson Walum, *The Dynamics of Sex and Gender: A Sociological Perspective* (Chicago: Rand McNally Publishing Company, 1977), pp. 139 and 140.

2. Ibid., p. 143.
3. Jane Baker Miller, *Toward a New Psychology of Women* (Boston: Beacon Press, 1976), pp. 88-95.
4. Ibid., p. 88
5. Ibid.
6. Jessie Bernard, *The Female World* (New York: The Free Press, 1981), p. 203.
7. Ibid., p. 205.
8. Ibid., p. 206.
9. Barbara G. Wheeler, "Accountability to Women in Theological Seminaries," *The Journal of Religious Education* 76, No. 4 (July-August, 1981), p. 389.
10. Ibid., p. 390.
11. Bernard, *The Female World*, p. 376.
12. Ibid., p. 376.
13. Elizabeth Langland and Walter Gove, eds., *A Feminist Perspective in the Academy* (Chicago: University of Chicago Press, 1981), p. 1.
14. Jack W. Carroll, Barbara Hargrove, and Adair T. Lummis, *Women of the Cloth* (San Francisco: Harper & Row, 1983), p. 209.
15. Ibid., p. 212.
16. Ibid.

Chapter 8

Human Development: Making Webs or Pyramids

HARRIET MILLER

"To be holy or perfect suggests more radical transformation and continued growth in the Christian life than can be captured by the idea of development."[1]

Stanley Hauerwas

Something happens to girls at eleven or twelve. Before the girls reach twelve they will probably hold out for their views, whereas the fifteen-year-old will probably yield. One of the questions that is raised is why does the younger girl believe in her own values and later discover that bringing in her values is going to make trouble. The older teens begin to watch for cues as to what their values ought to be. Carol Gilligan in her limited studies with women has discovered that the moral values of men and women are different and that male values of autonomy have been affirmed and the female values of connectedness have been devalued. From eleven years and for the rest of her life the girl goes ethically underground and keeps her view of connectedness of humanity as appropriate only in the "interpersonal sphere"—not the big world. Gilligan found that for girls and women to continue to trust their own ethical perspectives, the educational systems will have to stop thinking of female ideas as troublesome or trivial!

This chapter will attempt to review for religious educators some of the background that brought about the developmental stage theories. We will examine at which points the stage theories have omitted or distorted the experiences of women. The implications for changes in religious education will be projected and suggestions for further studies to document the proposals will be offered.

Education that truly transforms the persons is education of the imagination. Such education will continue to give encouragement to creativity and different styles of relationship. New patterns of development may allow the gifts and values that have been put underground by both males and females to bring liberation and new freedom that may be a necessity for the preservation of the world.

Developing the Theories

Since the time of Freud, whose works brought about a revolution in psychology, his mental structures concerning religion and femininity have been either rejected or widely used as hidden parts of later-stage structures of development. For Freud, Christianity and femininity are least valuable psychologically and culturally and the scientific attitude of ideal masculinity is most valuable.[2] Freud's misogyny has two poles: the negative qualities of femininity and the positive qualities of masculinity—related to fulfillment and the renunciation of wishes. Judith Van Derik points out in her study that renunciation of wishes is seen as the more valuable mental and cultural achievement. In reality principle thinking, a moral sense—a cultural achievement and scientific attitude—are traced to these renunciations. Freud sees fulfillment of wishes (bound to femininity) as militating against achievements. Freud also defines Christianity as fulfillment and the Mosaic tradition as renunciation. The wish to which Freud traces religious belief is the wish for paternal protection and consolation, so the illustration is of the existence of the paternal God.[3] "In Freud's conventional usage, femininity was associated with passivity, with the lack of a penis, with narcissism and with the traits of modesty, vanity, inclination to envy and jealousy, lack of social conscious or sense of social justice, a generally weaker moral sense (a weaker super-ego), inferior capacity for sublimation, greater disposition to neurosis, particularly to hysteria, a weaker sex urge, masochistic tendencies, earlier arrest of psychological development (rigidity), and an antagonistic attitude toward civilization as the enemy of family and sexual life."[4]

Freud's view of women was not refuted, and later theorists continued to look at women as a problem. Women were excluded from the theory-building studies. The omission of the experiences of women not only made the development stage theories inaccurate but it made the renunciation or separateness pattern of the males the norm for progress and achievement.

Developmental theories do allow us to speak of the dynamics of change and transformation and to focus on equilibrium and continuity. It is possible for the educator to describe predictable changes in formal terms. Each stage of development involves a basic transformation of the structure of the person's thinking and feeling. This transformation is the result of a process of interactions between the structure and the organism and the environment. Moral development is not changing one's point of view on a particular issue, but transforming one's reasoning and expanding one's perspective to include criteria for judging that were not considered previously.

The aim of education in moral judgment is to ensure the greatest development of each person. Piaget, taking a constructionist approach, proposed three stages in a child's moral judgment. The child moves from constraint into cooperation and from cooperation into generosity. As he began to study adulthood in relationships, there were varying degrees of constraint. The recognition of differences seemed to bring a mystical respect for rules, yet everyone followed his or her own game without paying much attention to his or her neighbor. Piaget's four stages leading up to adolescence were operational structures that constitute the thought processes at a given time. In the formal operational thinking, Piaget does emphasize reality thinking which Freud had labeled a result of renunciation or separation and attributed to the masculine. Piaget separates cognition or knowing from emotion or affection. He relegates intuition and imagination to the play world. There is neglect of the symbolic processes and no understanding of the role of imagination in knowing. The idea of separation or renunciation is recognized in most developmental texts. The reality of either intuitive thinking or continuing connection is lost or relegated to the background with women. Women are depicted as mired in relationships and not able to think objectively.

Erik Erikson worked out a psycho-social approach to development. Erikson described the role of persons in society. He saw human beings developing according to steps predetermined by the growing person's readiness for new interactions. He describes the life cycle as "repeating, embodying, and reexpressing the pattern of the generations." He has included caring in his life cycle. Women are included in the considerations. A woman's preparation for care is centered in her body which becomes a "protective abode and a fountain of food."[5] Erikson comes out of the Freudian tradition but is interested not so much in the individual as in the whole generation. The parent becomes a child again as the life cycle is repeated. This treatment of females makes them the nurturers and gives the aggressive role to the males. His terms *autonomy, initiative,* and *industry* are all described in male terms. The relational care and response to others is deleted in the progression. Jean Baker Miller asks the question, "Is it immaturity for children *not* to want to leave a world where people do care?" So females can find themselves in the trust relationships and in the intimacy period, but Erikson thinks intimacy in a woman comes before identity because her *name* is to depend on the man she is going to *marry.* In Erikson's view women need men to fill that empty "inner space." A woman holds off her identity to later identify with a man in relationship. Caring is not described until the generative adult stage (after both the identity crisis of adolescence and intimacy as delineated in the young adults between the self and other), then Erikson describes the universality of the need for compassion and care. When in his developmental stages Erickson charts a path where the sole precedent to the intimacy of adult relationships is the trust established in infancy and all intervening experience is marked only as steps toward greater independence, then separation itself becomes the model and the measure of growth.[6]

Piaget and Erikson both deal with development but in different ways. Piaget is a structuralist who sees the struggle for wholeness in the cognitive area. He provides a relational model that emphasizes the "world pole." Erikson emphasizes the self pole. Woman's place in man's life cycle has been that of nurturer, caretaker, helpmate, and the weaver of those networks of relationships on which she in turn relies. Women have taken care of men. Men have devalued that care. Concern with relationships appears as a weakness rather than a strength.

In 1960 Kohlberg began a study of fifty American *males,*

ages ten to twenty-eight. He interviewed this group for three years. From this data he developed a six-stage theory of moral development. Kohlberg believes that moral education and religious education should be separated. His fundamental principles and assumptions go directly against a theological approach and support a social science approach to religious education. Kohlberg believes that religion is not necessary or highly important for the development of moral judgment or conduct. He believes that the aim of all education should be based on the psychological data about how a person grows and learns. Kohlberg's stages do not tell us much about the relationship of thinking and feeling—about what happens to our thinking when we are emotionally involved in the dilemma. Kohlberg moves toward a single principle of justice which is made into a judgment or decision. At the adolescent period, Kohlberg's stage three marks the beginning of the conventional level of moral judgment. It is called "mutual interpersonal expectations, relationships, and interpersonal conformity." This stage is achieved by each person in the context of his or her interaction with others and with the help and guidance of the available contents of common sense and moral thought. Kohlberg relies heavily upon the cognitive structure of Piaget, and his latter stages are influenced greatly by Erikson. For a true ethical orientation of adulthood to develop, the identity crisis must have been resolved sufficiently to make possible caring and generativity toward others. It is in this transition from adolescence to adulthood that Carol Gilligan challenges whether the principle of justice is a sufficient basis for supporting even male's moral development during the next period—which Erikson describes as a "crisis of intimacy." Gilligan raises the question concerning the necessity of having a leap of faith in events where there is no rational certainty. This possibility would enable one to choose the best possible action among the available alternatives. She believes that Kohlberg has too uncritically bought rational absolutes. Commitments are deeply personal and hence relative to person, place, and culture. Kohlberg considers attachments as weakness and sees woman's moral weakness as manifest in an apparent diffusion and confusion of judgment. Gilligan sees this concern with relationships and responsibilities as women's moral strength. She says in women this subjective attachment itself follows three stages. These stages are: (1) egocentric (I don't want to be hurt); (2) self-sacrifice and responsibility (I don't want to hurt others); and (3) morality of nonviolence (I don't want to hurt myself or others).[7]

Stages of Faith Development

Since 1970 James Fowler has worked on stages of faith. Kohlberg feels that Fowler's broad definition of faith, which does not distinguish faith from moral judgment, leads to confusion. Fowler feels that education and nurture should aim at full realization of the potential strength of faith at each stage and at keeping the reworking of faith that comes with stage changes current with the parallel transitional work in psycho-social eras. At times when the lagging faith stage fails to keep up with psycho-social growth remedial nurture may be needed. In a few instances a precarious faith development outstrips or gets ahead of psycho-social growth. Help may then be needed in reworking the psycho-social functioning. The ethical development offers a dialogue possibility between morality and religion. Fowler considers his work as establishing the context for moral judgment. Cognition as shown in Piaget's stages is too narrow an example. Kohlberg expands a little in the opportunity. Erikson's influence has been more persuasive and subtle and this influence became a part of Fowler's mind-set in research of faith stages. Faith development studies confirm the judgment that human beings are gifted at birth with a readiness to develop in faith. Fowler's hope is that stages of faith will lead to enlarged commitment to be part of God's work of righteousness and faith liberation in our world. Faith stages meet the structural developmental criteria for stages. They provide generalizations and formal descriptions of integrated sets of operations of knowing and valuing.

Growth and development in faith also result from life crises, challenges, and the kinds of disruptions that theologians call revelation. James Loder believes that we live in transitions more than in the stages. He raises the question of transforming moments that do not fit into the stage theory, but allow for God's action in the growth of people.

Women's Development and a Different View of Moral and Faith Development

This quick review of the stage theories of human development has centered on moral and faith development at the beginning of the adolescent years. This particular period seems to show most clearly the difference between women and men in their responses to this study. Since women's experiences were not considered in most of the studies, we are now concerned to look at moral development by tracing the human development through shifts in the hierarchy of power relationships. It is possible that the dissolution of a hierarchy into an order of equality is an ideal vision of development. The conception of relationships in terms of hierarchies implies separation (renunciation) as the moral ideal where everyone stands alone—

independent, self-sufficient, connected to others by the abstractions of logical thought. There is a need to represent in the mapping of development a nonhierarchial image of human connection to show in the vision of maturity the reality of interdependence. This vision of a web of connection rather than building a pyramid-like hierarchy comes with the recognition of relationship that prevents making people fit into structures. It also prevents aggression and gives rise to the understanding that generates a capacity for responsibility and caring that is so needed in the world.

Carol Gilligan challenged the various developmental-stage theories because of the omission of women's experiences in their studies. She also pointed out the differences between two modes of describing relationship between other and self. She studied the relation between judgment and action in a situation of moral conflict and choice. Gilligan followed William Perry in asking for a more contextual vision which affirms the need for value commitments that transcend relativism, but also acknowledges that particular forms of commitment are deeply personal and hence both relative to person, place, and culture. Gilligan also is in search of a moral stage beyond justice at which the individual will take moral responsibility for her action—not because she can logically establish its rightness, but because she knows that in the absence of rational certainty one still has to risk the best possible action. The failure of women to fit the existing models of human growth may point to a problem in the representation—a limitation in how the theorists conceive the human condition or an omission of certain truths about life. If women are not adequately represented in the studies, it certainly makes the results less than valid. If the theorists are still either accepting the Freudian view of women or are unable to image mutuality between men and women, the results of the study as well as the original selection of the participants could make the stages inaccurate. Educators have wished for clear maps of development.

Carol Gilligan did three studies to challenge the adequacy of the treatment of gender in development studies. She did a study about self and morality with twenty-five college students. She also used the abortion issue with twenty-nine women to study experiences of conflict and choice. A third study dealing with rights and responsibilities was done to refine the different modes of thinking about morality and their relation to different views of self. There were one hundred forty-four male and female participants matched for age, intelligence, education, occupation, and social class at nine points across the life cycle. A specially chosen sub-sample of thirty-six collected data on conceptions of self and morality, experiences of moral conflict, and choice and judgments of hypothetical moral dilemmas. Gilligan points out that the studies have been valuable, but the data were not complete in previous studies.

Gilligan and Developmental Studies

In the rest of this chapter some of the areas of these developmental studies will be discussed in light of Carol Gilligan's findings. We will also give some educational implications for this additional view.

The first question addressed was the place of women in a male life cycle. We have already indicated that Freud considered women to be inferior because of their attachments (relationship) to the masculine renunciation (separation patterns). Chodorow (in 1974) felt that the differences in the sexes came because women have been largely responsible for early child care. This concludes that feminine personality is derived in relation and in connection to other people. Robert Stoller defined gender identity as the unchanging core of personality formation.

Gender is with rare exception firmly and irreversibly established for both sexes by the time the child is around three. Females bond with mothers in a close relationship. Mothers experience boys as the male opposite. The relationship from the beginning is different. Mothers often expect boys to become strong and to separate early. The individuation for the boys begins at once as the mother curtails their primary love and sense of empathetic tie. Boys are encouraged to be "big" and "strong" with a more emphatic individuation and a more defensive establishing of ego boundaries. For boys, separation and individuation are inseparable. Masculinity is defined through separation. As a result, males may have difficulty with relationships.

For the girls, the mother sees them as an extension of themselves. Girls develop with a basis for empathy already well established. Femininity is defined through attachment. Females tend to have problems with individuation. This failure to separate is defined as women's failure to develop. Girls learn early that safety is found in human connections where clear boundaries in established and safe distances limit aggression, whereas boys tend to see others as equal to the self and that equality makes some connection safe. Boys do not wish to come into close relationships because they fear entrapment. Development for girls means, that they see themselves in an expanding network of connection and attachment and through the web of close relationships comes the discovery that separation can be protective and need not bring them to isolation.

Women feel threatened by rule-bound competitive achievement situations because these events may break the web of connection. For men the rules and the structured competition give a limit to aggression and thus appear comparatively safe. The paradox concerning separation and attachment is that we know ourselves as separate only insofar as we live in connection with others and that we experience relationship only insofar as we differentiate the other from self. Women's development is a fusion of identity and intimacy. Attachment and separation are the base of the life journey. In the infant development, attachment and separation are the patterns most likely to be established. In more recent times, some parents have tried to direct their children toward both connections and separation or behavior that leads to both identity and intimacy.

Educational Implications in Early Years

1. Teachers need to examine their own assumptions about competitive patterns and patterns of giving praise so that affirmation goes to group-supportive behavior rather than to particular persons.
2. Girls in mixed-group situations need more experience in taking initiative as leaders or as planners for the group. This can only be helpful if the behavior is interpreted as a contribution to the group's goal rather than putting emphasis on the persons who are skilled.
3. Teachers need to be aware of their responses to the boys and to the girls. They need to check to see if their responses fit into the pattern established in the hierarchical chain where masculine values are superior and feminine values are inferior. Teachers need to form a group sharing of each other's opinions and statements concerning their own sexist attitudes and their value orientation.
4. Boys need to be encouraged to empathize, to express feelings, to learn to show their own sense of their image.

There needs to be reflection and discussion to eliminate stereotypic phrases such as: "Boys don't cry," or "Girls can't think logically."

5. Teachers and pupils must learn how to recognize issues in everyday encounters that are related to both identity and intimacy. They must also learn how to move from competition for status to a mutuality of goals and programs.

6. Questions that need to be raised: How does one perceive the statement concerning the first three years of life and the mind/attitude set by that time? Do we put our emphasis on the group or on individuals? What relationship with the home is required to enable permanent lifestyle change?

More research is needed to discover how determinative is the pattern of the early years. More research is needed to determine more definitively whether individuation and relationship are learned patterns or if they are inherent in males and females.

Patterns of Winning and Losing

Observations of children at play and in structured games during their elementary years (ages ten through eleven) give insight into the differences in winning and losing. Boys play outdoors more. They tend to play in large, age-heterogenous groups using competitive games more. Their games last longer because they resolve differences by an elaboration of the rules. Even though there are quarrels throughout the games, they develop a set of fair procedures. Boys tend toward roles that have arisen out of resolving disputes. Certain members of the group can be depended upon to take the role of the other, and the structure becomes safe and supportive. Boys tend to learn the independence and the organizational skills necessary for coordinating large groups. This fits them for assertive roles in other groups. Boys deal with competition by playing with their enemies and competing with their friends.

Girls of this age play indoors more. They form best-friend dyads and play turn-taking games. They tend not to be as openly competitive. They have more difficulty settling disputes quickly because they have been conditioned not to quarrel. They are more willing to end the game and keep their relationships intact than to risk quarrels. The girls are more tolerant about the rules, are more easily reconciled to innovation. Piaget feels that girls are less logical or have less legal sense. Their play and relationships exhibit sensitivity and care for the feelings of others. This sense of the others can impede later expectations that they must be "one of the boys" to succeed. Later, girls must choose between being "like a man" or being dependent upon men. But their play and actions before the age of eleven do not indicate those choices. The play is more cooperative and less given to the abstraction of roles in human relationships.

Dealing with Conflict

Women tend to work contextually concerning conflict. They respond contextually, beginning with responsibility to others and then moving to responsibility for self. They seek solutions inclusive of everyone's needs. Conflict is responded to with acts of caring and ways to improve the whole situation.

Men enter conflict situations categorically thinking of responsibilities to self and then considering the intent of their responsibility to others. Rules are established to limit interference and thus to minimize hurt. Men think in larger structural terms and then first ignore the immediate relationships. Responsibility to the group entails a limitation of actions to fit the rules. There is a restraint of aggression to protect autonomy. Reciprocity is a pattern of retaining status and autonomy in the group—"not losing face." The bargaining often has mathematical equations. They tend to see the world as dangerous confrontation and explosive connections. Responsibility implies not doing what he wants to do because he must think of others.

Educational Implications

1. Teachers in planned experiences may need to examine their procedures to see if their process is more competitive or shows more cooperative and mutual use of gifts.
2. Teachers may need to check to see if there are opportunities in the groups for caring, concern, and empathy and if opportunities are brought to the surface and affirmed.
3. The skills of dialogue and conflict management can help to move both boys and girls to less destructive ways of settling disputes. They must be modeled in actual situations in the classroom and playground.
4. The use of playing to help gain empathy for the particular other is important. This points to learning the art of distinguishing differences without creating feelings of hostility or superiority. This requires a language that does not use "up-down" words, such as "persons who are above or over us," "climbing the ladder of success," "those actions are beneath us."
5. A hierarchical ordering of values and relationships determines winners and losers. Teachers and students may opt to change their goals to indicate a network of connections. Such a web of relationships sustained by a

process of communications would give many more op-
tions and many more reasons for participation.

Puberty: A New Individuation

Young men and women arrive at this stage in their lives
with a different interpersonal orientation and a different
range of social experiences. Freud said that adolescence is
a time of repression again. He said that it is necessary for
women to change their "masculine sexuality" into "feminine sexuality." He describes women as becoming passive
and accepting of their role as nurturer and helpers of men.
According to this hierarchical patterning, she becomes
aware of the "wound to her narcissism" which leads her to
develop the "proper sense of inferiority." Erikson expects
development to be at the point of identity by the beginning
of adolescence. Gilligan suggests that girls arrive at adolescence either psychologically at risk or with a whole different agenda and often conform to a serving role instead of
seeking their own identity. The task for both young men
and women at this stage is to gain a strong sense of self, to
strengthen an identity that can span the changes of puberty. Out of this task comes the adult capacity to work and
love in mutuality. Erikson's first event centered in relationship, but the next three centered in individuation: His
event two—autonomy vs. shame and doubt is leading to
separateness and renunciation; event three—initiative vs.
guilt leads to separateness and achievement. Girls and boys
will be at different places because the girls will not compete for status or productivity as much. Erikson is setting
up a norm that fits a male child. He became aware that it is
different for girls. As we have seen, he sees that she holds
her identity in abeyance in this period so that she can
attract a man by whose name she will be known and by

whose status she will be defined. These ideas were produced by Erikson in 1968. Many changes have begun to affect this view in the last twenty years, yet each new generation still finds residual evidence of this attitude. Females carry on relationships as a part of identity. She is known *in,* not necessarily *by* her relationships.

Boys come into puberty often with no preparation for intimacy because they have spent so much of their energy in developing autonomy and finding their productivity. Only trust vs. mistrust (Erikson's) have suggested any cooperation or mutuality in their experiences. Freudian thinking indicates that the pleasure principle related to fulfillment must be sacrificed to a reality principle. He suggested it was best achieved by analysis in psychoanalytic care. According to that pattern "to renounce wish" is to progess in development. Religion is considered a wish-fulfilling illusion in his pattern. Development for girls would then imply losing the sense of imagination, wishful thinking, and creativity. In this pattern, femininity takes on the qualities of objectivity, passivity, castration, and masochism. The father as the castrating figure becomes a symbol for God and all authority.

The period called latency period is a period in which a boy comes through a great trauma in first being his father's rival or later having his father as lover. In either case he will be castrated. His challenge is to learn better ways of establishing both individuality apart from parents and connectedness with people of different patterns. That challenge could be partially met by including women's experience of fusing identity and intimacy—finding oneself in relationships. Women need to own their own experiences. Finding a language of relationship itself is a difficult task. Women are caught between an underground world that sets them apart from others, because they are developing at a different pace, and a world of connections that sets them apart from themselves. Their task is to find out that responsiveness to self and responsiveness to others are connected in the same web rather than opposed to each other. Both the hierarchy of relationships of status and role and the web of connectedness are imbedded in the cycle of human life.

Educational Implications

1. Working in small groups which change often enough to provide skills in initiating new connections and in entering and leaving intimate groups is a necessary process for adolescence.
2. Providing opportunities for team work, (mixed boys and girls) by giving recognition on contributions rather than on persons with particular skills is helpful. It would be best to evaluate by measuring the contribution to the total group.
3. Learning the skill of honest and constructive evaluation to dispel the tendency to "play games."
4. Teachers and parents can best work together on the process of changing roles and connections in the family and close groups where appropriate.
5. Understanding the relationship of wish (intuitive thinking) and logic (formal operations) helps persons see the necessity of the forms of right and left brain thinking.

Conflict and Success

Women tend to develop a fear of success. The anticipation of success in competitive achievement activity, especially against men, produces anticipation of certain negative consequences; for example, threat of social rejection and loss of femininity. Women's orientation is personal so that they may not want positions. Women have qualifications and self-doubts about their public speaking. They are afraid of divided judgment which indicates lack of precision. The gift which women could bring is to expose the limited views of success that the culture sets up. They could choose a more wholistic view of fulfillment in life. Feminine strength is an overriding concern in relationships and responsibility and this could be the fulfillment.

Men show a readiness to adopt and celebrate a rather narrow vision of success. Their orientation is positional. They have played by the rules and won. Success gives them a status in the group and in their own view. But this leaves them with a fear of close relationships.

Educational Implications on Success

1. Teach with clear definition of success as a way to assess progress toward a goal. Encourage persons to see both personal goals and group goals as the indication of success.
2. Provide adequate checkpoints for achievement for those persons who need motivation from frequent checkpoints and position, but keep the process clear with flexibility in changing goals to fit contextual shifts and needs.
3. Provide frequent observation and reporting of the group's ability to decide, proceed, and evaluate accurately.
4. Avoid having autonomous thinking, decision making, responsible action, or expressive activities linked with only one sex. Be sure that all persons have equal opportunity to participate and be evaluated in each area.
5. Point out the unhealthy split between work and love—

affirm the interdependence of love and caring with decisive judgments.
6. Understand the contribution of the feminine view of relationship as a legitimate goal.

Self and Morality

Moral decision is the exercise of choice and the acceptance of responsibility for that choice. When women perceive themselves as having no choice, they excuse themselves; making these choices brings women privately into conflict with the conventions of femininity as it has been defined as passive and dependent. The subtle moral equation for women is for goodness with self-sacrifice. Women have avoided making judgment of others, but they have both judged themselves and been judged in their care and concern for others. The conflict in reclaiming the self comes between showing compassion and seeking autonomy, between virtue and power. Women attempt to solve moral problems in such a way that no one is hurt. For men, morality is often conceived in interpersonal terms. They consider the problem objectively. For women, goodness is equated with helping and pleasing others. If women are to progress in the patterns of moral development suggested by Kohlberg, they must enter into this objectivity and learn to live by rules and principles in Kohlberg's higher stages.

It is the strength of women in care and sensitivity that marks them as deficient in moral development. To learn to live by men's rules means to change the way they think about responsibilities and rights. The concept of morality as justice ties development to the logic of fairness, equality, and reciprocity. How the decision is made depends upon the self-concept. For women the thinking about moral decisions is contextual and narrative rather than formal and abstract. Instead of centering on fairness according to rights and rules, the tendency is to think about relationships and responsibilities. There is a strong sense of being responsible to the world, person to person, rather than to make a universal declaration of human rights. They consider it an omission not to help others when one could help them. The more objective view is to be concerned about interfering with people's rights. Women bring to the life cycle a different point of view and a different order of priorities. Women's place in men's life cycle is to bring an injunction to care, a responsibility to discern and alleviate the real and recognizable trouble.

The contribution of men is the injunction to respect the rights of others and thus to protect people from interference and the right to life and self-fulfillment.

The development theories carry on a litany of celebration of separation, autonomy, individuation, and natural rights. Only when theorists have lived with women's experiences as long as they have with men's experiences will these theories become correspondingly more fertile.

One of the areas that surfaces in the moral decisions is the presence of violence in establishing order. Women see more violence in impersonal situations of achievement than in situations of affiliation. The danger in achievement is isolation, fear that in standing out in judgments or achievement they will be left alone.

Men see more violence in situations of personal affiliation than in situations of achievement. Intimacy brings the possibility of entrapment or betrayal, being caught in a smothering relationship or humiliated by rejection or deceit. Violence results from the sense of being caught in a situation.

Virtue for women lies in self-sacrifice. Women's development pits goodness against questions of responsibility and choice. The women feel strongly the conflict between self-ishness and responsibility. The current depictions of adult development fail to describe the progression of relation-ship toward a maturity of interdependence. Early adults move away from absolutes. Women move from an absolute of care (not hurting anyone) to a need for personal integri-ty. They continue to make a claim for equality, then em-bodied in rights. A change in the understanding of relationships transforms the definition of care.

Men in the same periods move from absolutes of truth and fairness (equality and reciprocity) to finding differ-ences between self and others. The next step relativizes equality in the direction of equity and an ethic of generos-ity and care. Both men and women following this growth and progression as described by William Perry will come to a new understanding of responsibility and choice.

Language of responsibilities provides a webline of rela-tionships to replace a hierarchical ordering that dissolves with the coming of equality. The language of rights under-lines the importance of including in the network of care not only the other but the self.

Educational Implications

1. Teaching by the use of narratives, case studies, directed observation in the context will help to combine judg-ment and mercy, caring and rights.
2. Helping women to understand and act upon a self-con-cept of adequacy and an ability to judge is important in teaching. This development of self-concept comes from involvement in decision-making situations, not only from telling persons about themselves.
3. Teachers help by encouraging an image of true ser-

vanthood in a balanced view with self-sacrifice. Women need help so that they do not lose themselves in serving.
4. Teaching by modeling a balance between giving and receiving is important. In the classroom that means a balance between giving information and hearing from the students. This experience will help persons be willing to receive from others.

Summary

In this chapter most of the critique of the developmental theories is taken from Carol Gilligan's views concerning the differences in the stages of development for women. She has suggested three levels of experience for women. The suggested levels are:

1. Tenuous concept of self—a question of survival of self is at stake and a conflict between the images in society concerning femininity and adulthood.
2. Women's self-concept includes doing the right thing by society's standards. This corresponds to the stage of conformity, and for women goodness is defined by self-sacrifice. Survival now means the acceptance by others. Modes of dependence or manipulation are used to survive.
3. A transition to an inward acknowledgment of self and acceptance of responsibility for her own judgments.

These levels indicate the struggles that are precipitated when women are judged by norms set in the male experience rather than in a balanced experience from both men and women. A marriage between the adult development as it is currently portrayed and women's development as it begins to be seen with more studies of women's experience could lead to a new understanding of human development and a more generative view of human life. Founded to be a community of peers, all sons and daughters of the same God, we are beginning to see the need for new symbols of unity that are circular or web-like and not pyramidal—symbols that combine skills that are expressive and functional in the same units.

NOTES

1. Stanley Hauerwas, *A Community of Character*, as quoted in Lindsy Van Gelder, "Carol Gilligan: Leader for a Different Kind of Future," *Ms. Magazine* (January, 1984), pp. 37ff.
2. Judith Van Herik, *Freud on Femininity and Faith* (Berkeley: University of California Press, 1982), p. 107.
3. Ibid., p. 18.
4. Ibid., p. 20.
5. Erik Erikson, *Insight and Responsibility* (New York: Norton, 1964), p. 132.
6. *Harvard Educational Review*, No. 48 (1978), p. 509.
7. Carol Gilligan, *In a Different Voice* (Cambridge, Mass.: Harvard University Press, 1982), p. 105.

Profiles of Contributors

RUTH FLOYD completed her undergraduate degree at the University of Toledo at the same time her son, Kendall, and daughter, Karen, were attending high school and college. While completing her degree she worked as a church secretary and continued her volunteer work with the youth of Maumee United Methodist Church. Her call to full-time ordained ministry came out of this experience, and she received her Master of Divinity and Master of Arts in Christian Education from The Methodist Theological School in Ohio. Ruth is presently serving as one of the pastors for Bexley United Methodist Church in Columbus, Ohio.

JOANMARIE CONROY SMITH, C.S.J., currently Associate Professor of Christian Education at The Methodist Theological School in Ohio, received her Ph.D. in philosophy from Fordham University. For a number of years she taught philosophy at St. Joseph's College in New York. She is the author of *Morality Made Simple (But Not Easy)*, co-author of *Modeling God*, and *Death: The Night Between Two Days*. She has also published a number of articles on feminist issues.

JUDITH ANDERSON DORNEY has been doing religious education for fourteen years on both the junior high and high school levels. She is currently working in St. Clement High School in Somerville, Massachusetts, where she teaches as well as directs the high school's Youth Ministry Program. She has published both essays and book reviews in religious education journals and newsletters. She received a B.S. from Nazareth College in 1969 and an M. Ed. from Boston College in 1984.

REGINA COLL is a sister of St. Joseph, Brooklyn, New York. She is presently the Acting Director of Field Education of the Theological Department at Notre Dame University. She is the co-author of *Death: The Night Between Two Days,* and she edited *Women and Religion.* She has lectured on women's issues in this country, in India, and the British Isles. Her Ph.D. is from Union Theological School and Columbia University.

JANET TANAKA has been involved in music and adult religious education for more than twenty years. A member of the Baha'i Faith, she has written and taught extensively on interfaith concerns, especially those of women. Janet was the first member of her faith and the second non-Christian to be elected to the board of directors of the Center for the Prevention of Sexual and Domestic Violence, a unique organization that deals exclusively with training clergy and religious counselors to handle these issues within the framework of their own faith and in the education of secular counselors to the importance of the religious concerns of victims and abusers. She heads a national ad hoc committee preparing training materials on abuse and violence counseling for the Baha'i Faith. In addition to her numerous popular articles and research papers in both earth science and religion, Janet is also the author of a disaster novel: *Fire Mountain,* and a folk mass, *Creation Alleluia!* Although her undergraduate degree is in Human Development (in counseling and psychology), Janet's interest in religious issues concerned with domestic violence stems from her own experience as a former victim of the kind of misinterpreted Christian doctrines and un-Christian behavior she discusses in her chapter.

ETHEL JOHNSON is Director of Field Education and Professor of Church Administration at The Methodist Theological School in Ohio, Delaware, Ohio. She previously served on the staff as educator of three local parishes in urban settings. She served as Associate Executive Secretary of the New York East Conference Board of Education, United Methodist Church. She has served extensively in denominational Lay Ministries and Conferences on Polity and Education. She has served in Sierra Leone and Nigeria and emphasizes the life and power of the laity. She has published articles and studies in denominational curriculum. M.T.S. and M.R.E., Hartford Seminary.

FERN MOLLOHAN GILTNER has been a religious educator at least since receiving a M.R.E. from Andover Newton Theological School. She has been a religious educator in churches and has taught in ecumenical workshops and schools. She is currently the consultant and supervisor in Christian education at The Methodist Theological School in Ohio, Delaware, Ohio.

HARRIET MILLER, currently Professor of Christian Education at United Theological Seminary, Dayton, Ohio, received a Ph.D. in education at The Ohio State University. She has previously served as a religious educator in local churches, denominational conferences, and councils of churches. She has also worked extensively on boards and agencies and commissions of The United Methodist Church. She has published articles in denominational and professional journals and a chapter in *Introduction to Christian Education*. She has lectured on and actively encourages the recognition of the role of women in religion.

Index of Names

Index of Subjects